Alfred's Basic Piano Library

Group Piano Course

A Course designed for
Group Instruction using
Acoustic or Electronic
Instruments

Theory

Ear Training

Sight Reading

Ensemble

Technique

Rhythm Drills

Composition / Improvisation

Cover illustration and interior art by Martin Ledyard

Willard A. Palmer, Morton Manus, Amanda Vick Lethco
Adapted by Gayle Kowalchyk and E. L. Lancaster

Alfred

Preface

A Note to Students and Parents

You are beginning an exciting adventure with piano lessons. Music study develops performance skills as well as an appreciation of a fine art. Improved coordination, a broadening of interests, a discovery of the importance of self-discipline and a world of pleasure are additional rewards from study.

Regularity in practice is important. At beginning stages, several short practice times each day are more important than one long practice session. Children in cooperation with parents should establish regular practice times for each day. Parents have the responsibility of showing an interest in the child's progress. Patience, sincere praise, enthusiasm for new material and occasional participation in music making at home will be beneficial to the student.

The fact that you have chosen group lessons for your study brings increased motivation for lessons. Students are encouraged and challenged by other group members. The joy of making music with others occurs on a regular basis. We offer our best wishes to you in your new adventure. It will be exciting and richly rewarding!

A Note to Teachers

Welcome to *Alfred's Basic Group Piano Course!*

This course is designed specifically for young students who are beginning piano study in a group setting. It also can be used with students who have a combination of group and private lessons. Book 1 introduces keyboard basics in a format especially designed for group instruction.

The book is divided into units. Each unit includes a variety of activities in areas designed to create a comprehensive musician and pianist. New concepts are introduced using motivating music. These concepts are reinforced with written theory, ear training, sight reading, rhythm drills and composition/improvisation exercises. Students in the group should stay together in the book but some teachers may want to supplement with individual performance repertoire for each student, to address varying ability levels. The book is designed to give the teacher maximum flexibility in lesson planning.

This book is fully supported by two Compact Discs and two Standard MIDI File (SMF) disks. Students will want to own the Compact Discs for home practice, and teachers will want the MIDI disks for use in the classroom. Each example in the text that contains an accompaniment is identified by an icon that shows the disk number and TRACK number for the example: ◄))) GM/CD 1-1(45). The first number after the icon denotes the CD/SMF disk number. The second number is the TRACK number on the CD and the Type 0 MIDI file on the SMF disk. The third number (in parentheses) is the TRACK number of the Type 1 MIDI file on the SMF disk. Accompaniments range from simple drum patterns to full orchestrations. These accompaniments add musical interest and motivate students to complete assignments both in the classroom and at home. The CDs and MIDI disks also contain the ear training examples so that students may complete them in the group or at home during practice.

An exciting game, *Musical Adventures*, is available that was specially created to reinforce the concepts presented in the course. This game adds motivation and enthusiasm to classroom activities.

A *Teacher's Handbook* for the book serves as an aid in curriculum development and daily lesson planning. The handbook contains suggested lesson plans and teaching tips; assignments follow each lesson. It also recommends ways to use the *Musical Adventures* game in the classroom. These plans were specifically created for average age beginners (ages 7–9) and provide a starting point for teachers to adapt for individual classes. It also suggests ways to successfully integrate keyboard and computer technology into the curriculum.

Upon completion of this book, students will be ready to begin *Alfred's Basic Group Piano Course, Book 2.* We hope these pages will help you open the door to the wonderful world of music to many students.

How to Sit at the Piano

SIT TALL!

Lean slightly forward.

Arms hang loosely from shoulders.

Elbows a little higher than keys.

Bench facing piano squarely.
Knees slightly under keyboard.

Feet flat on floor, if possible.
Right foot may be slightly forward.

You may place a book or stool under your feet
if they do not reach the floor!

SIT HIGH ENOUGH!

If you do not have a piano stool that moves up and down,
you may need to use a book or a cushion to have the
correct position!

Fingers Have Numbers

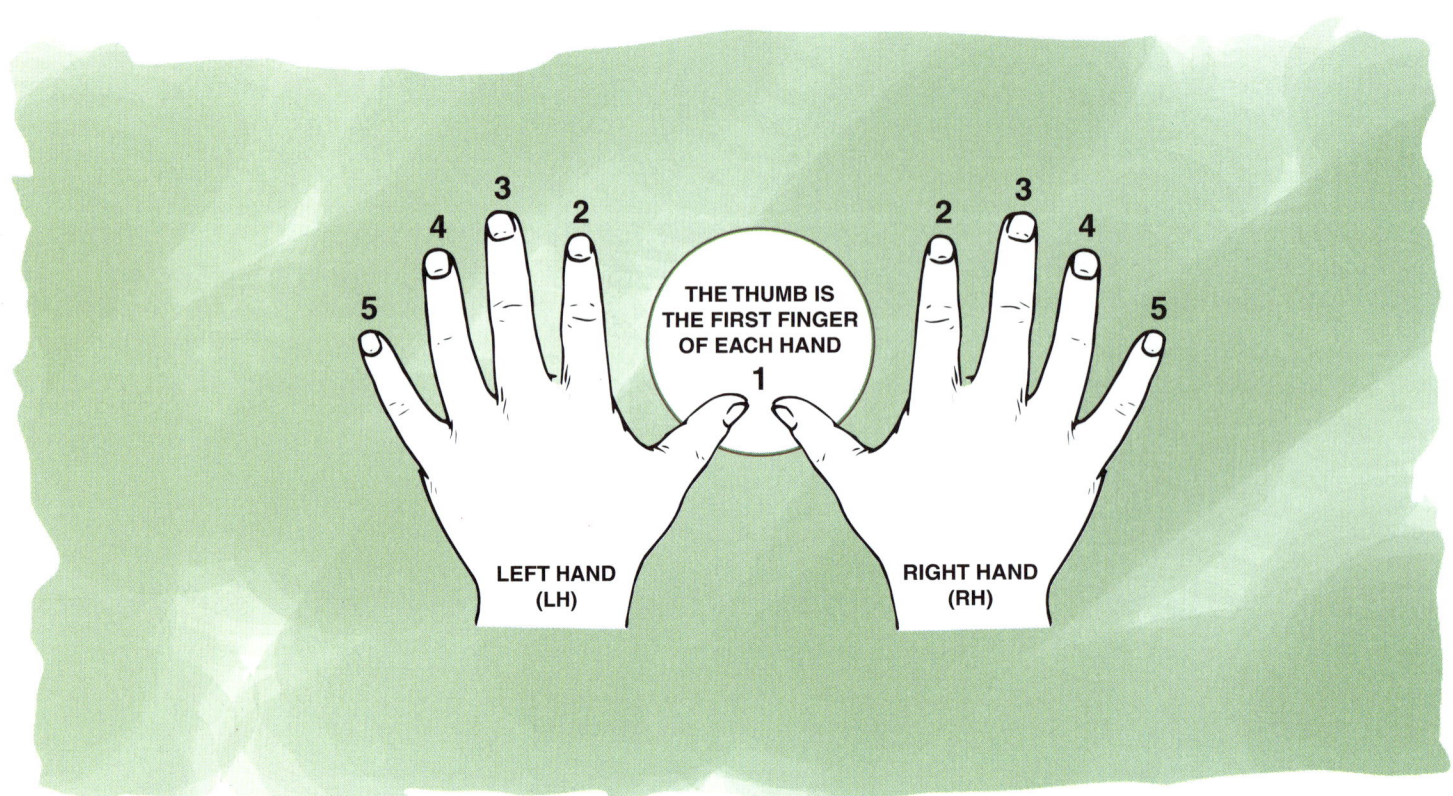

THE THUMB IS THE FIRST FINGER OF EACH HAND
1

LEFT HAND (LH)

RIGHT HAND (RH)

1. Your teacher will draw an outline of your hands on the inside cover of this book.

2. Number each finger of the outline.

3. Hold up both hands with wrists floppy.

- Wiggle both 1's
- Wiggle both 2's
- Wiggle both 3's
- Wiggle both 4's
- Wiggle both 5's

Your teacher will call out some fingers for you to wiggle.

Piano Tones

When you drop into the key with a LITTLE weight, you make a SOFT tone.

When you use MORE weight, you make a LOUDER tone.

Always Curve Your Fingers!

Straight fingers have different lengths!

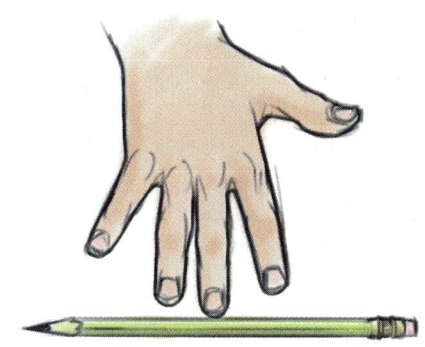

Curved fingers can have the same lengths!

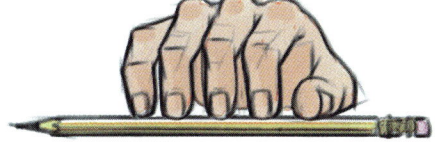

Pretend you have a bubble in your hand.
Hold the bubble gently, so it doesn't break!

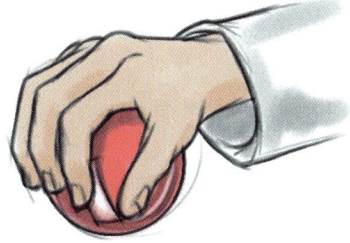

1. Play any white key with the 3rd finger of either hand, softly.

2. See how many times you can repeat the same key, making the tone a little louder each time you play.

Before you play any key you should always decide how soft or loud you want it to sound.

For the first pieces in this book, play with a MODERATELY LOUD tone.

Always LISTEN CAREFULLY to the music you are making!

The Keyboard

The keyboard is made up of white keys and black keys.
The black keys are in groups of 2's and 3's.

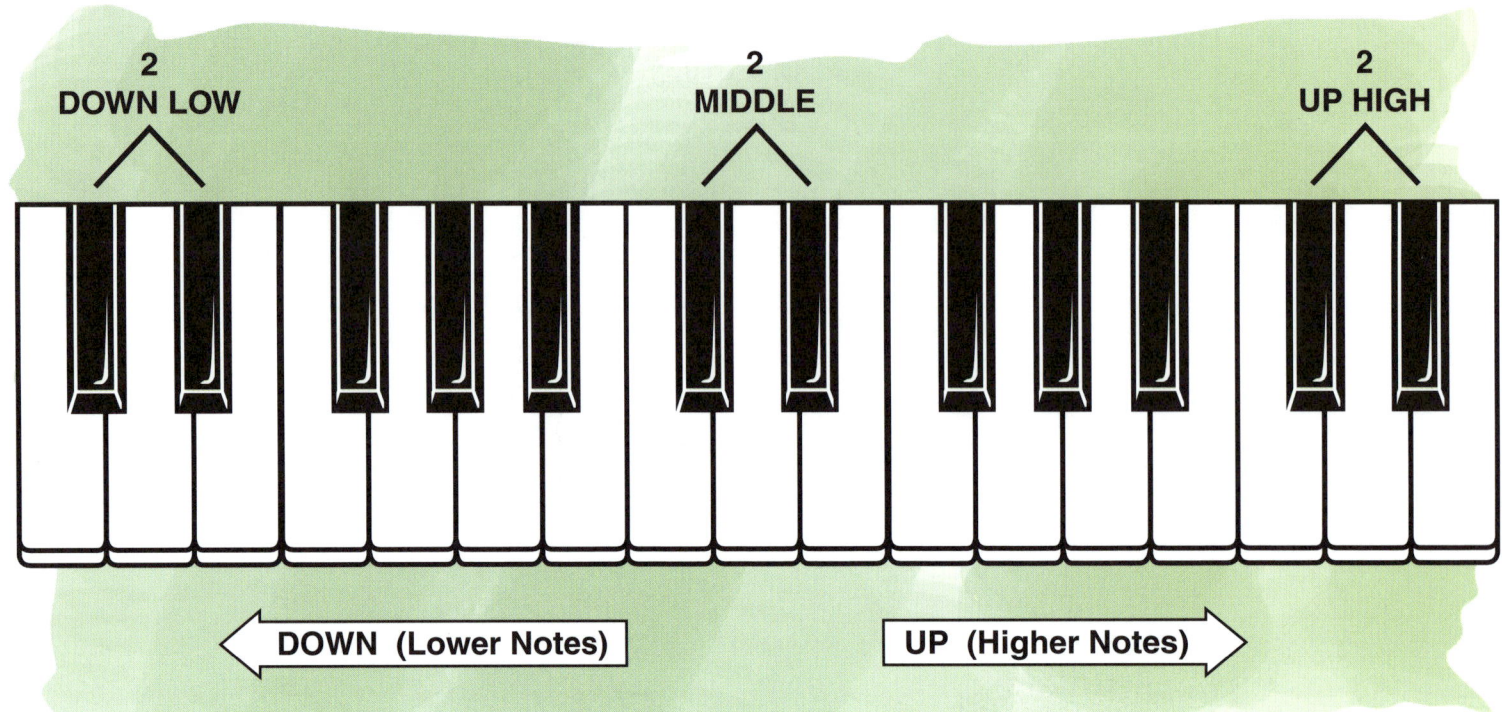

2 DOWN LOW   **2 MIDDLE**   **2 UP HIGH**

DOWN (Lower Notes) ← → UP (Higher Notes)

LH

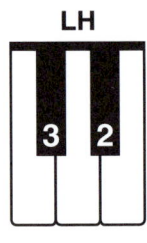

1. Using LH 2 3, begin at the middle of the keyboard and play all the 2-black-key groups going ◁ DOWN (both keys at once).

2. Play them again, one key at a time.
PLAY: LH 2 3.
SAY: "Step down" as you play each pair.

RH

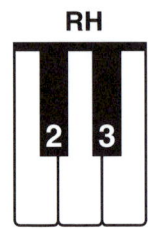

3. Using RH 2 3, begin at the middle of the keyboard and play all the 2-black-key groups going UP ▷ (both keys at once).

4. Play them again, one key at a time.
PLAY: RH 2 3.
SAY: "Step up" as you play each pair.

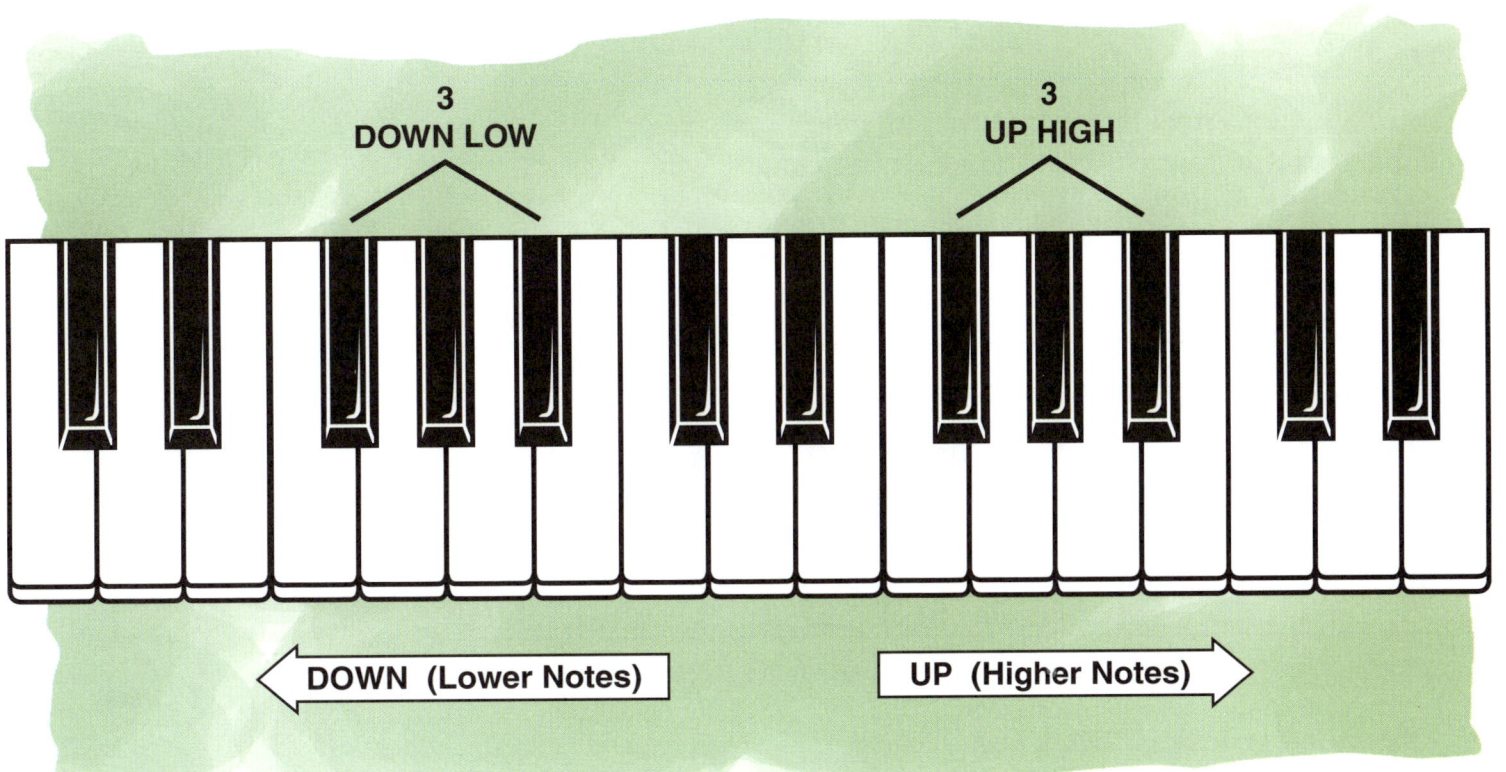

3
DOWN LOW

3
UP HIGH

DOWN (Lower Notes)

UP (Higher Notes)

LH

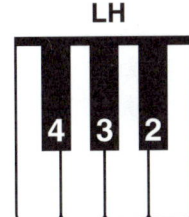

1. Using LH 2 3 4, begin at the middle of the keyboard and play all the 3-black-key groups going ← DOWN (all 3 keys at once).

2. Play them again, one key at a time.
PLAY: LH 2 3 4.
SAY: "Step - ping down."

RH

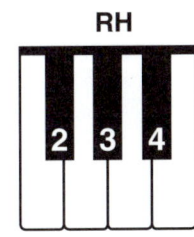

3. Using RH 2 3 4, begin at the middle of the keyboard and play all the 3-black-key groups going UP → (all 3 keys at once).

4. Play them again, one key at a time.
PLAY: RH 2 3 4.
SAY: "Step - ping up."

Theory

The Keyboard

As you have just learned, the keyboard is made up of white keys and black keys. The black keys are in groups of 2's and 3's.

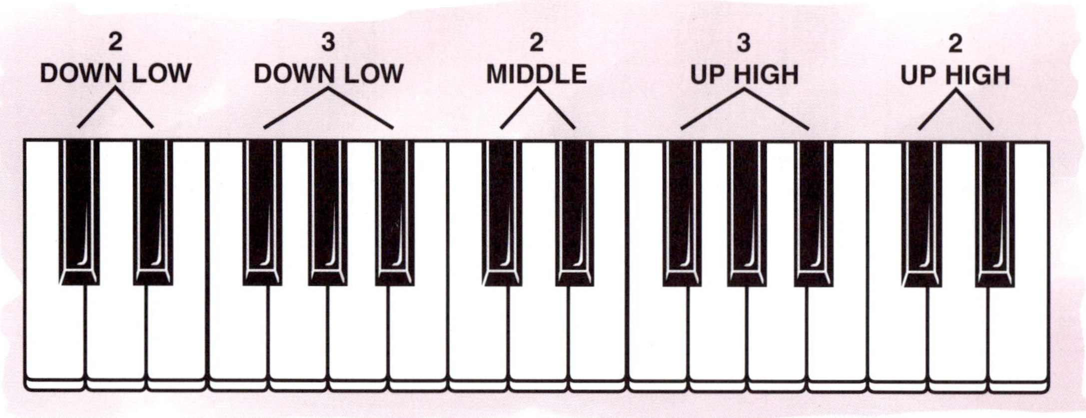

| 2 DOWN LOW | 3 DOWN LOW | 2 MIDDLE | 3 UP HIGH | 2 UP HIGH |

1. Fill in the groups of 2 black keys.

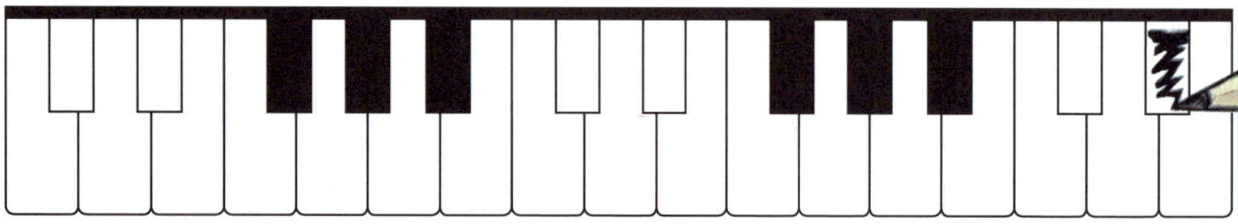

2. Fill in the groups of 3 black keys.

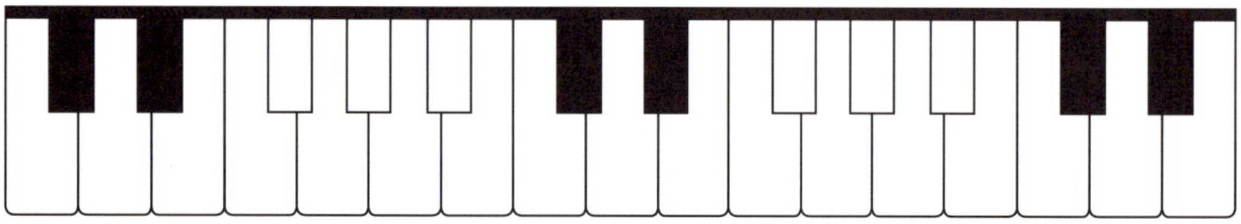

3. Draw a circle around each group of 2 black keys.

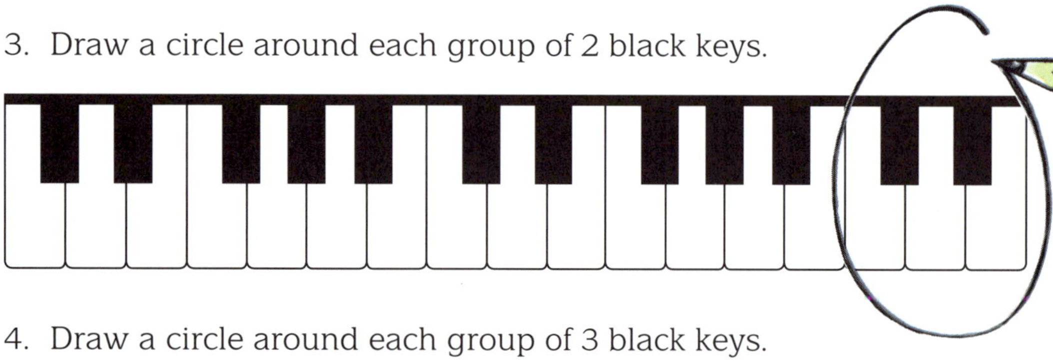

4. Draw a circle around each group of 3 black keys.

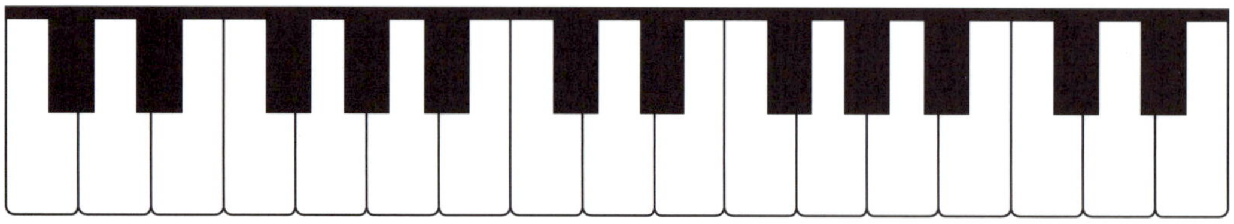

Ear Training

Low Sounds and High Sounds

1. Your teacher will play LOW and HIGH sounds.
   - Circle LOW if you hear LOW sounds.
   - Circle HIGH if you hear HIGH sounds.

2. Your teacher will play sounds that go UP or DOWN.
   - Circle the arrow pointing up if the sounds go up.
   - Circle the arrow pointing down if the sounds go down.

🔊 GM/CD 1-1 (45)

1a
HIGH
Low

1b
HIGH
Low

1c
HIGH
Low

1d
HIGH
Low

🔊 GM/CD 1-2 (46)

2a
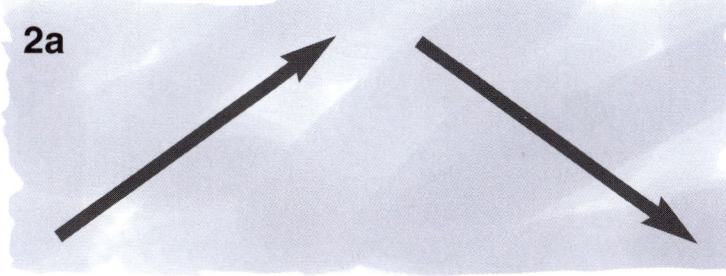

2b
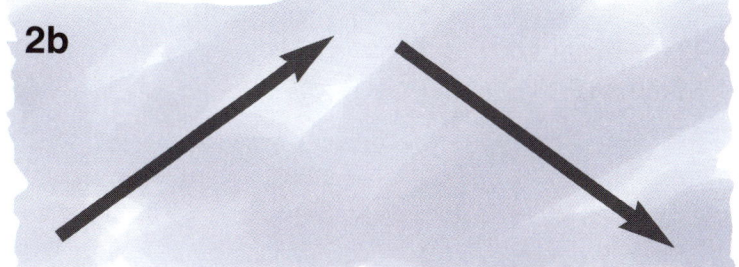

2c
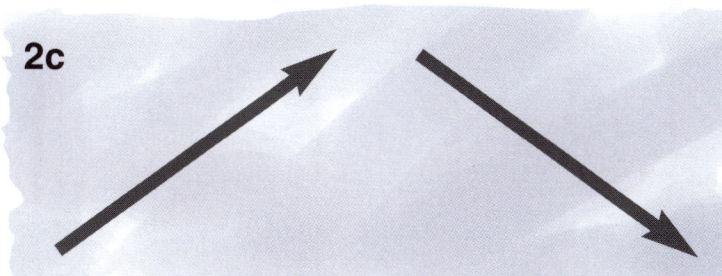

2d
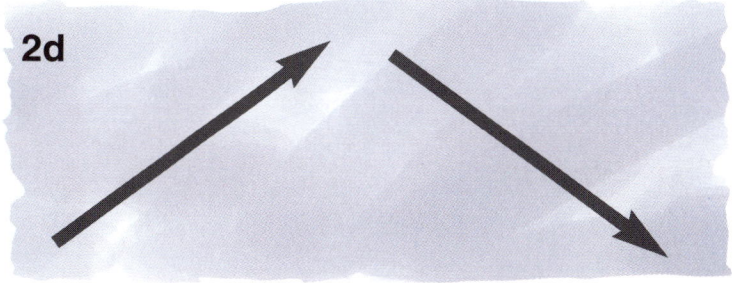

TEACHER: See page 79.

Quarter Note

a **short** note.

COUNT: "One"
OR: "Quarter"

Music is made up of **short** tones and **long** tones.

We write these tones in **notes,** and we measure their lengths by **counting.**

When we clap or tap **ONCE** for each note, we call it clapping or tapping the **RHYTHM.**

Clap or tap the following rhythm, counting aloud.

BAR LINES divide the music into equal **MEASURES.**

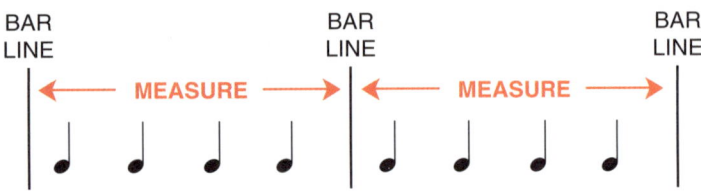

Right & Left

1. Clap (or tap) ONCE for each note, counting aloud.

2. Play & say the finger numbers.

3. Play & sing the words.

🔊))) GM/CD 1-3 (47)

POSITION OF HANDS

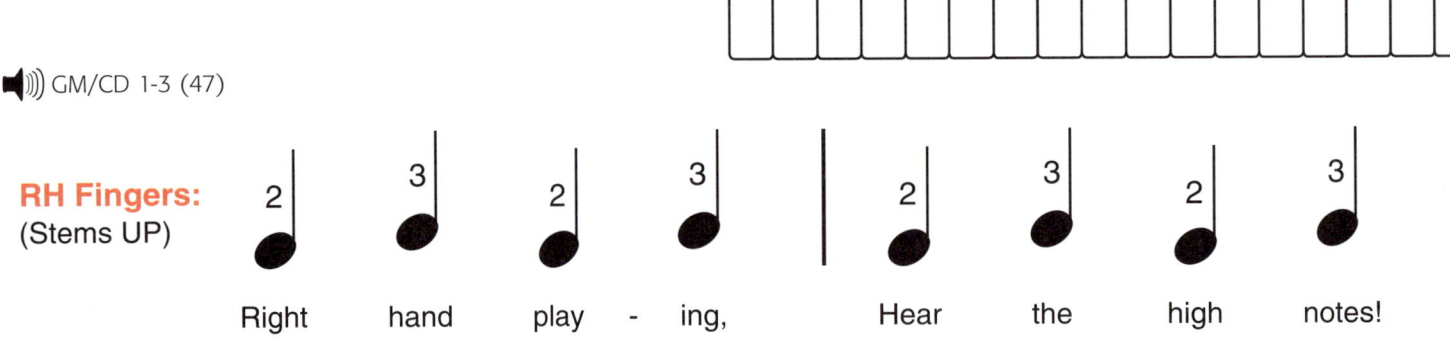

RH Fingers:
(Stems UP)

2	3	2	3	2	3	2	3
Right	hand	play	- ing,	Hear	the	high	notes!

3

DOUBLE BAR
used at the end.

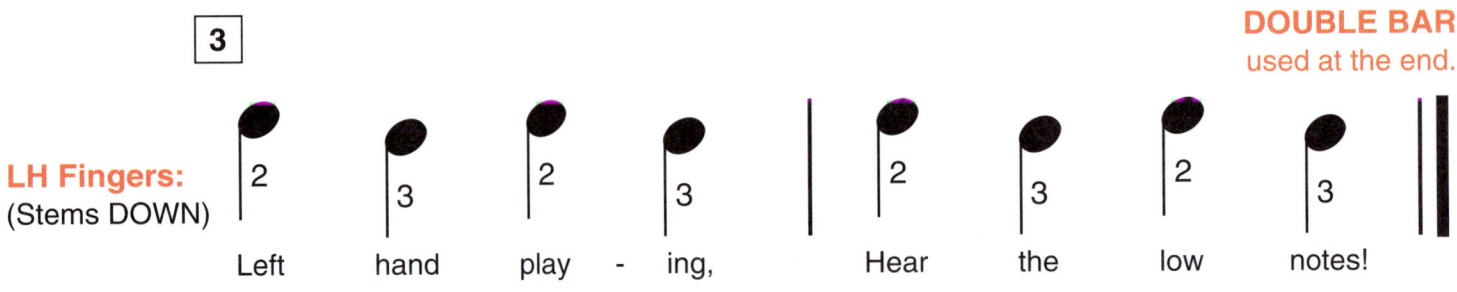

LH Fingers:
(Stems DOWN)

2	3	2	3	2	3	2	3
Left	hand	play	- ing,	Hear	the	low	notes!

Half Note

a **long** note.

COUNT: "One-two"
OR: "Half-note"

Clap (or tap) the following rhythm.

Clap **ONCE** for each note,
counting aloud as you clap.

Left & Right

1. Clap (or tap) the rhythm, counting aloud.

2. Play & say the finger numbers.

3. Play & sing the words.

POSITION

🔊 GM/CD 1-4 (48)

LH Fingers:
(Stems DOWN)

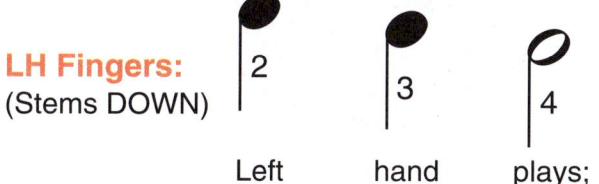

Left   hand   plays;

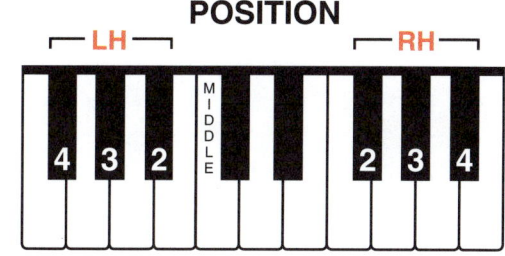

Sing   a - long!

RH Fingers:
(Stems UP)

3

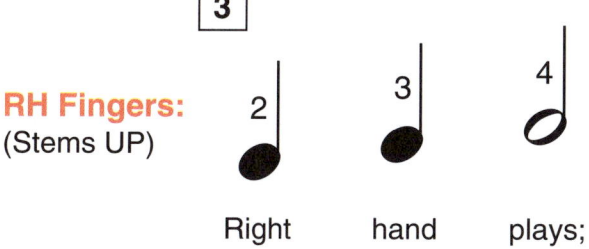

Right   hand   plays;

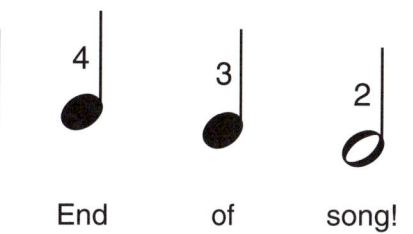

End   of   song!

Technique

With LH 2 3, begin at the middle of the keyboard and play all the 2-black-key groups going DOWN, using the indicated rhythm and finger numbers (one key at a time). Use the keyboard diagram as an aid to moving down the keyboard.

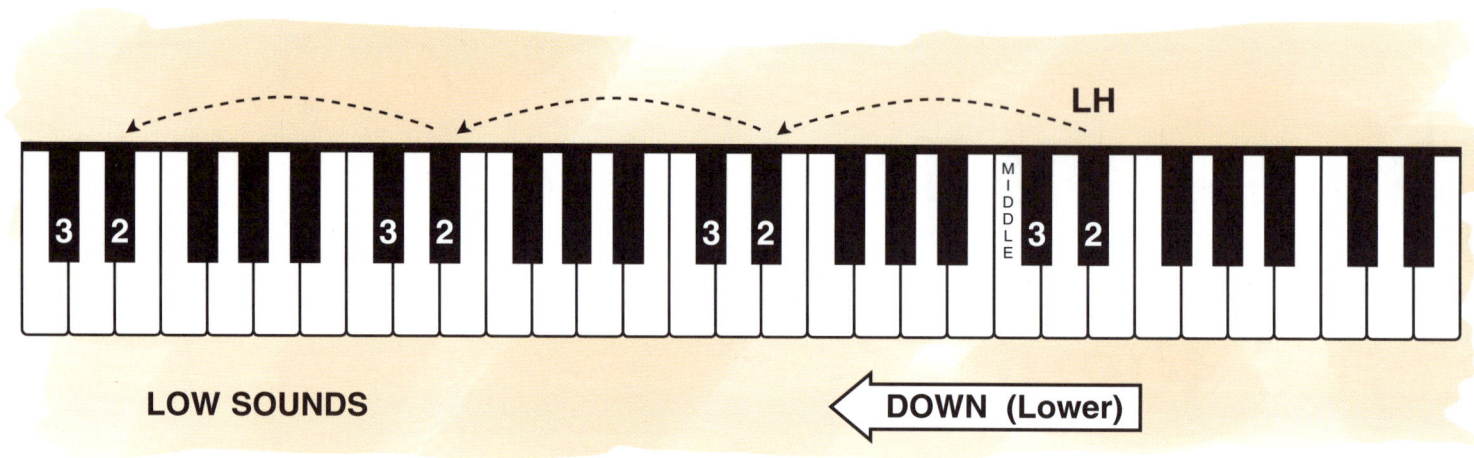

LOW SOUNDS   ⟵ **DOWN (Lower)**

GM/CD 1-5 (49)

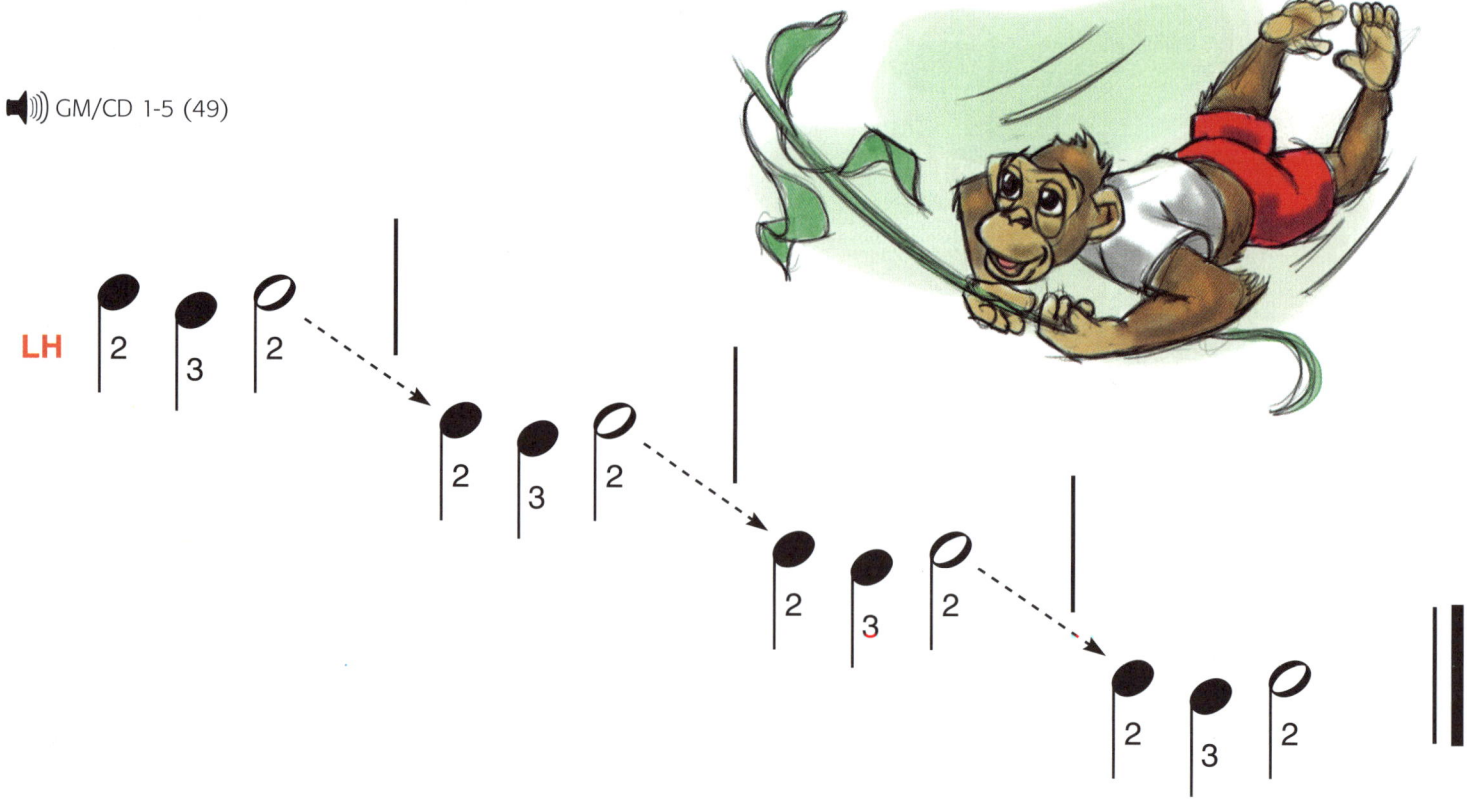

With RH 2 3, begin at the middle of the keyboard and play all the 2-black-key groups going UP, using the indicated rhythm and finger numbers (one key at a time). Use the keyboard diagram as an aid to moving up the keyboard.

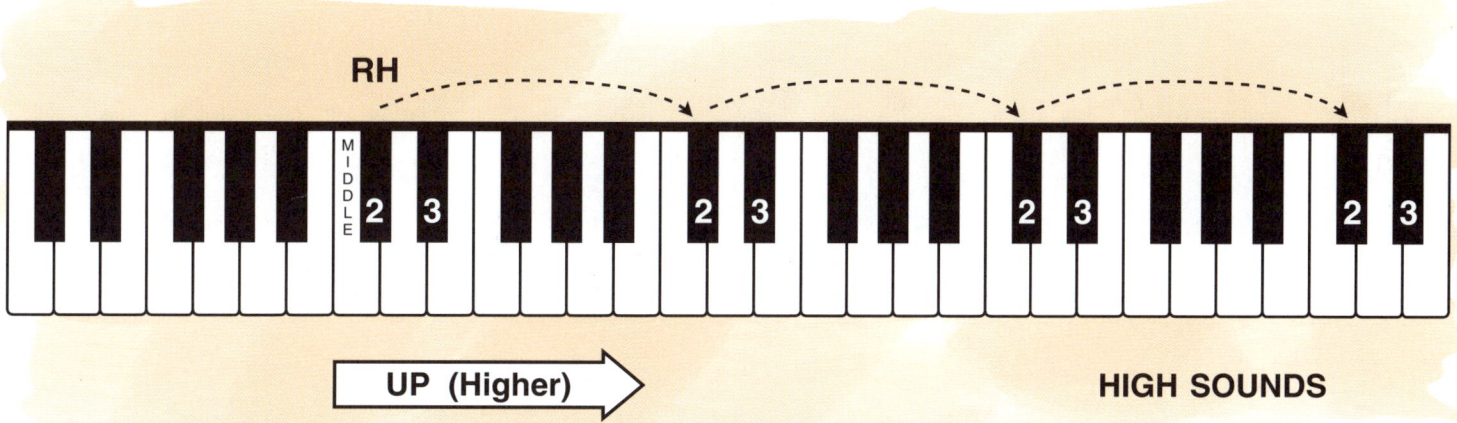

UP (Higher) ➡️   HIGH SOUNDS

🔊 GM/CD 1-6 (50)

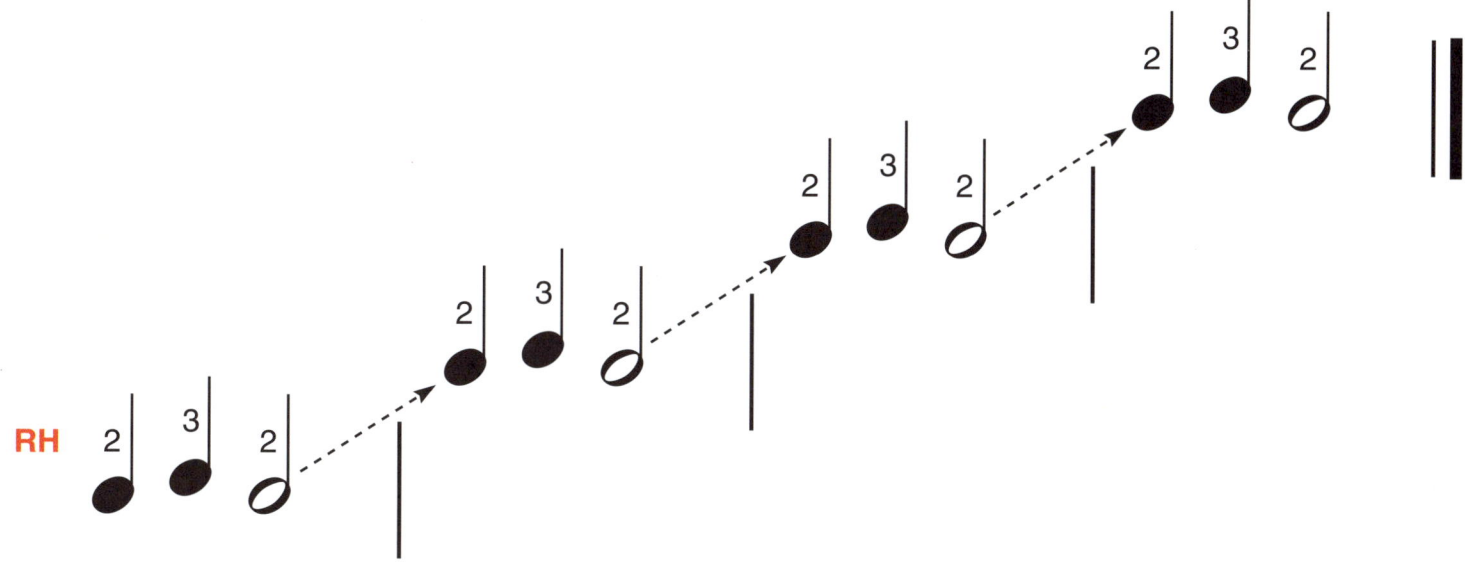

Rhythm Drills

Clap (or tap) the following rhythms, counting aloud.

GM/CD 1-7 (51)

a.

GM/CD 1-8 (52)

b.

GM/CD 1-9 (53)

c.

Composition / Improvisation

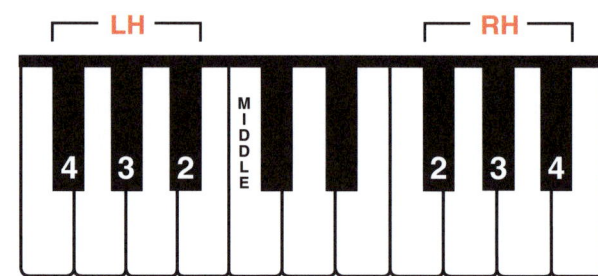

1. Create melodies in the given position using the rhythm pattern below. Begin and end each line with the given finger numbers.

2. Write the finger number below each left hand note and above each right hand note for your favorite melody.

GM/CD 1-10 (54)

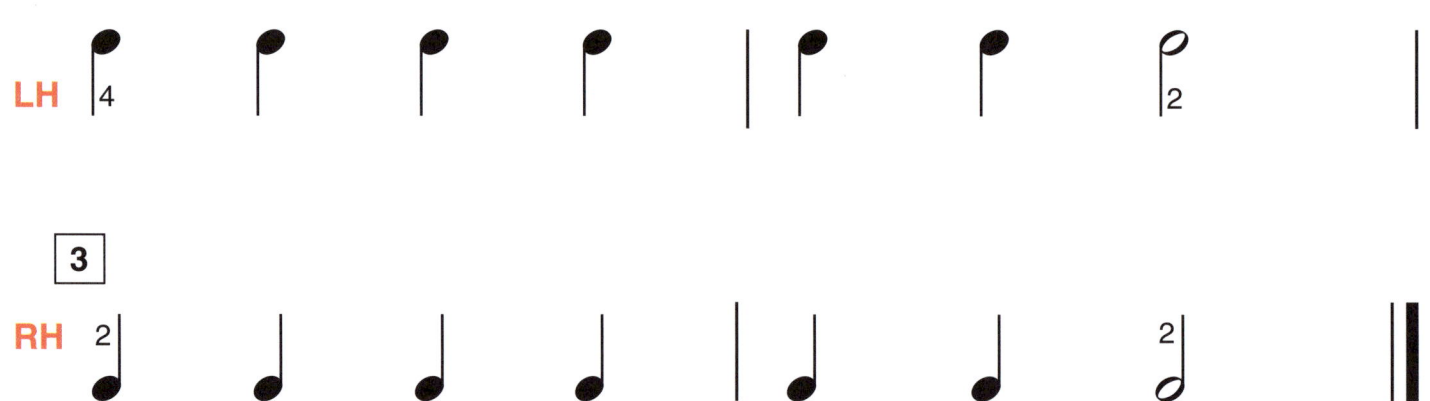

Whole Note — a **very long** note.

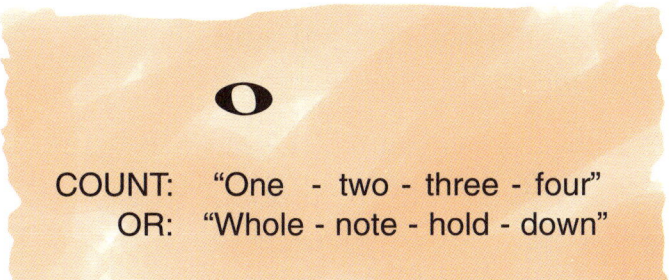

COUNT: "One - two - three - four"
OR: "Whole - note - hold - down"

Clap (or tap) the following rhythm.

Clap once for each note, counting aloud as you clap.

Merrily We Roll Along

1. Clap (or tap) & count.
2. Play & count.
3. Play & sing the words.
4. Play a duet with your teacher.

POSITION

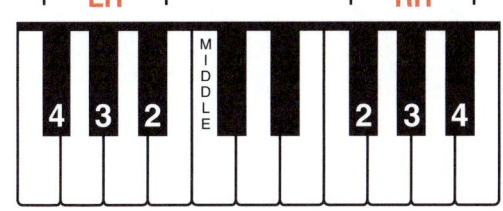

GM/CD 1-11 (55)

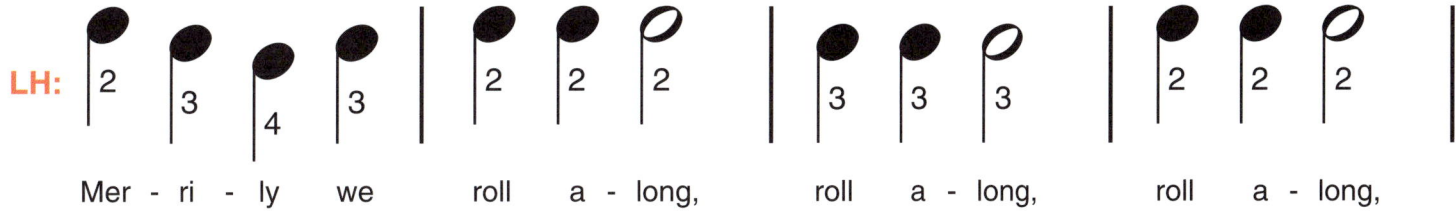

LH: 2 3 4 3 | 2 2 2 | 3 3 3 | 2 2 2

Mer - ri - ly we roll a - long, roll a - long, roll a - long,

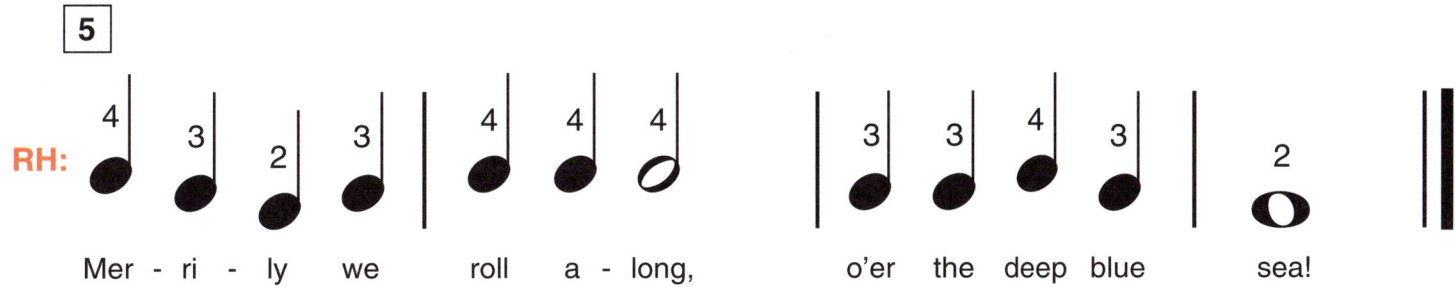

RH: 4 3 2 3 | 4 4 4 | 3 3 4 3 | 2

Mer - ri - ly we roll a - long, o'er the deep blue sea!

DUET PART (Student uses black key groups ABOVE the middle of the keyboard.)

Ear Training

Quarter, Half and Whole Notes

1. Your teacher will clap a rhythm pattern. Circle the pattern that you hear.

2. Your teacher will clap a rhythm pattern using QUARTER, HALF and WHOLE notes. Draw the missing note (♩ or ♩ or 𝅝) in the box.

GM/CD 1-12 (56)

1a

1b

1c

1d

GM/CD 1-13 (57)

2a
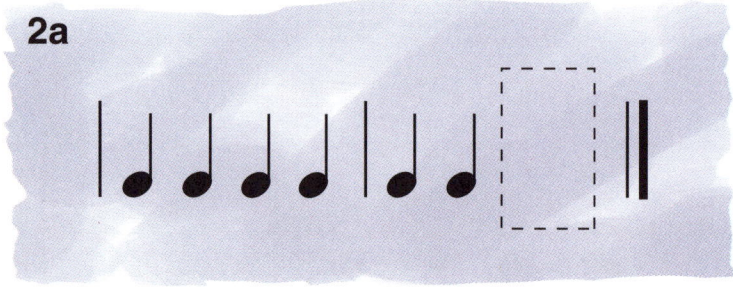

2b
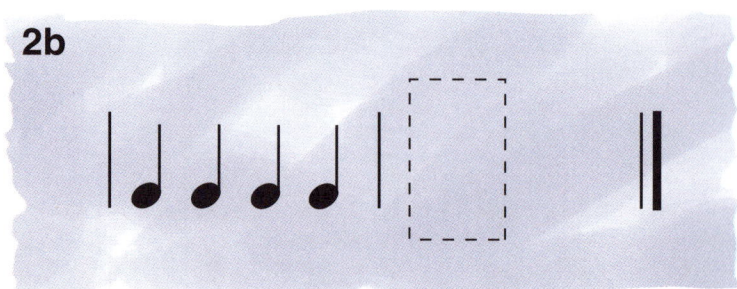

2c
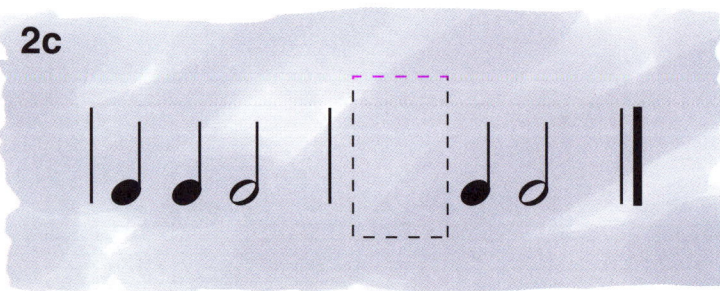

2d

TEACHER: See page 79.

UNIT 2 MORE KEYBOARD BASICS

Dynamic Signs

Handbells

1. Clap (or tap) & count.

2. Play & count.

3. Play & sing the words.

4. Play a duet with your teacher.

GM/CD 1-14 (58)

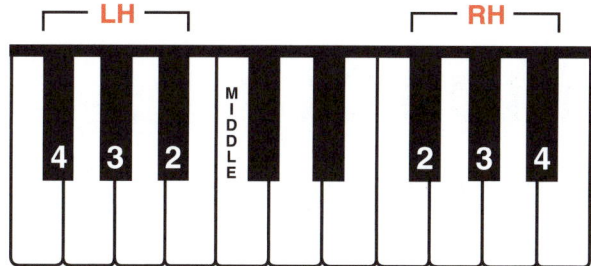

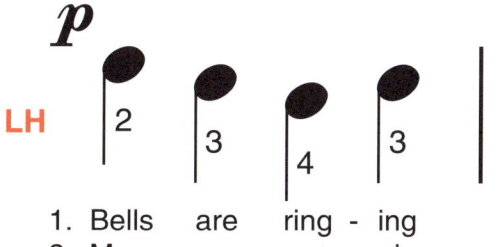

LH

1. Bells are ring - ing   sweet and clear,   Ding, dong,   ding, dong!
2. Mer - ry mu - sic   fills the air,

TWO DOTS
mean go back to
the beginning and
play again.

| 5 |

RH

Hap - py sounds for   all to hear,   Ding, dong,   ding!
Joy - ful sounds are   ev - 'ry - where,

DUET PART

8va throughout

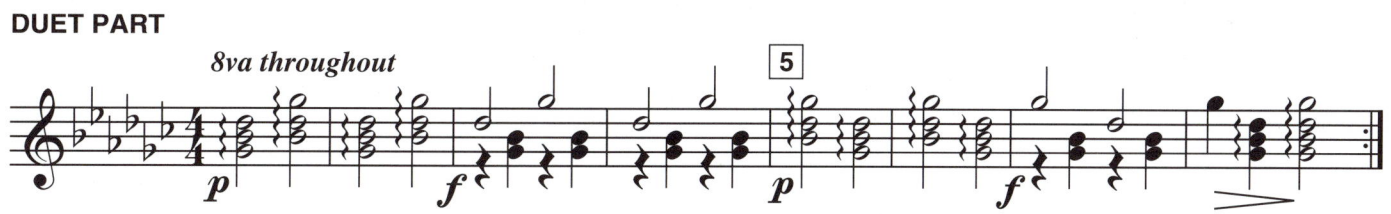

Theory

Please Play Two Times!!

TWO DOTS before a DOUBLE BAR :‖ means the music before the double bar must be played TWO TIMES!

So... go back to the beginning and **REPEAT!**

Pierrot

A PIECE FOR LEFT HAND

🔊 GM/CD 1-15 (59)

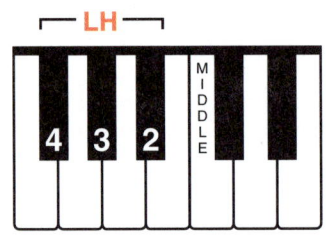

1. In the music below, add a DOWN stem to each note except the last.

2. Clap (or tap) & count.

3. Write a dynamic sign (𝒇 or 𝒑) in the box.

4. Play with LH.

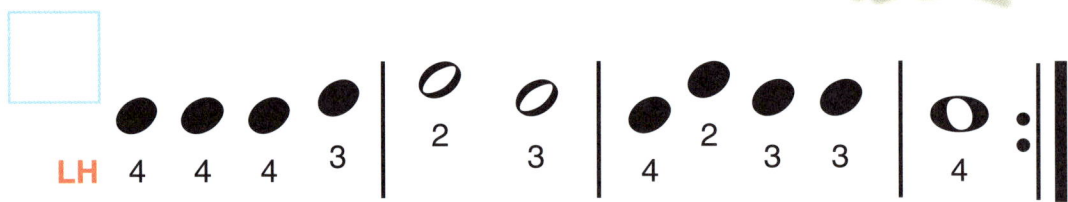

1. When you play this   mu - sic,   Dear Pier-rot, my   friend,
2. Two dots mean start   o - ver,   Play it once a - gain!

A Riddle

A PIECE FOR RIGHT HAND

🔊 GM/CD 1-16 (60)

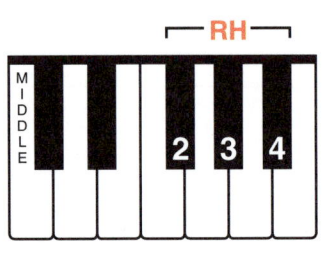

1. In the music below, add an UP stem to each note except the last.

2. Draw a sign after the last note which tells you to REPEAT the piece.

3. Clap (or tap) & count.

4. Write a dynamic sign (𝒇 or 𝒑) in the box.

5. Play with RH.

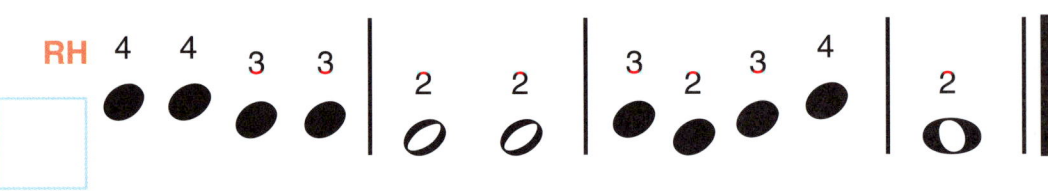

1. Here's a fun - ny   rid - dle;   It's a - bout this   song.
2. What has just four   meas - ures,   But is twice that   long?

Answer to Riddle:

This song, 4 measures repeated = 8 measures.

Sight Reading

1. Clap (or tap) & count.
2. Play finger numbers in the air & count.
3. Play & count.

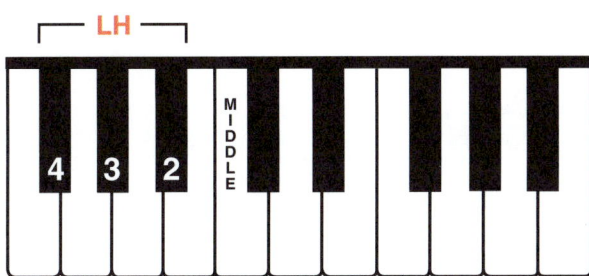

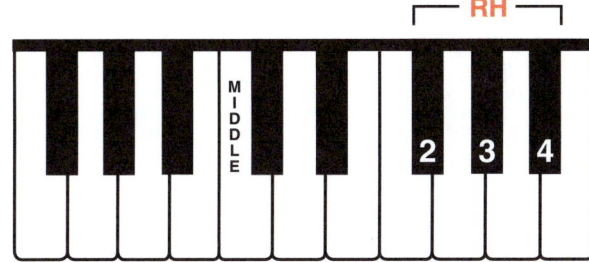

 GM/CD 1-17 (61)

 GM/CD 1-18 (62)

a.

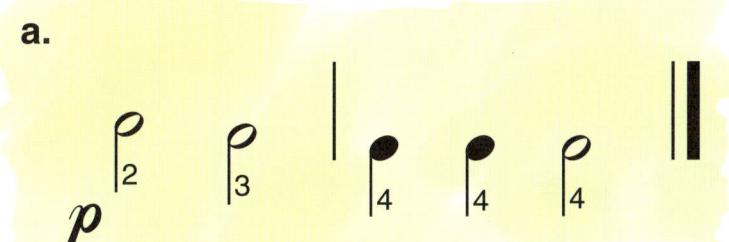

b.

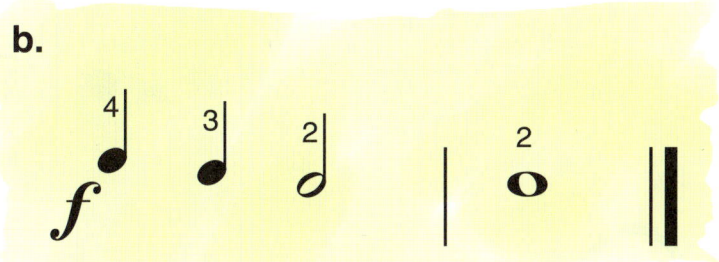

GM/CD 1-19 (63)

GM/CD 1-20 (64)

c.

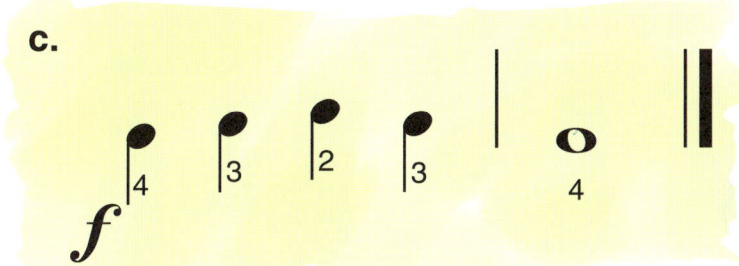

d.

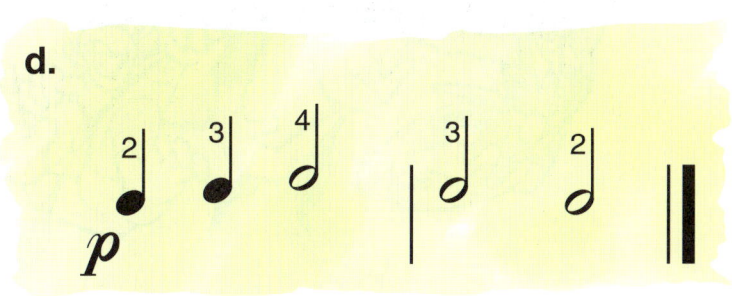

19

UNIT 2 MORE KEYBOARD BASICS

Technique

With LH 2 3 4, begin at the middle of the keyboard and play all the 3-black-key groups going DOWN, using the indicated rhythm and finger numbers (one key at a time). Use the keyboard diagram as an aid to moving down the keyboard.

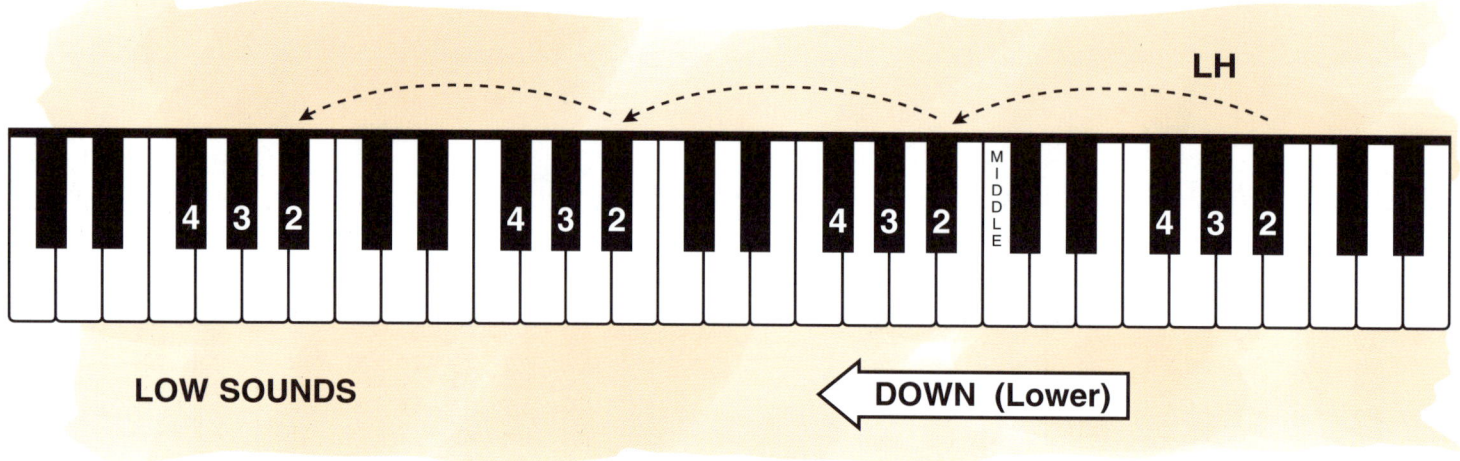

GM/CD 1-21 (65)

With RH 2 3 4, begin at the middle of the keyboard and play all the 3-black-key groups going UP, using the indicated rhythm and finger numbers (one key at a time). Use the keyboard diagram as an aid to moving up the keyboard.

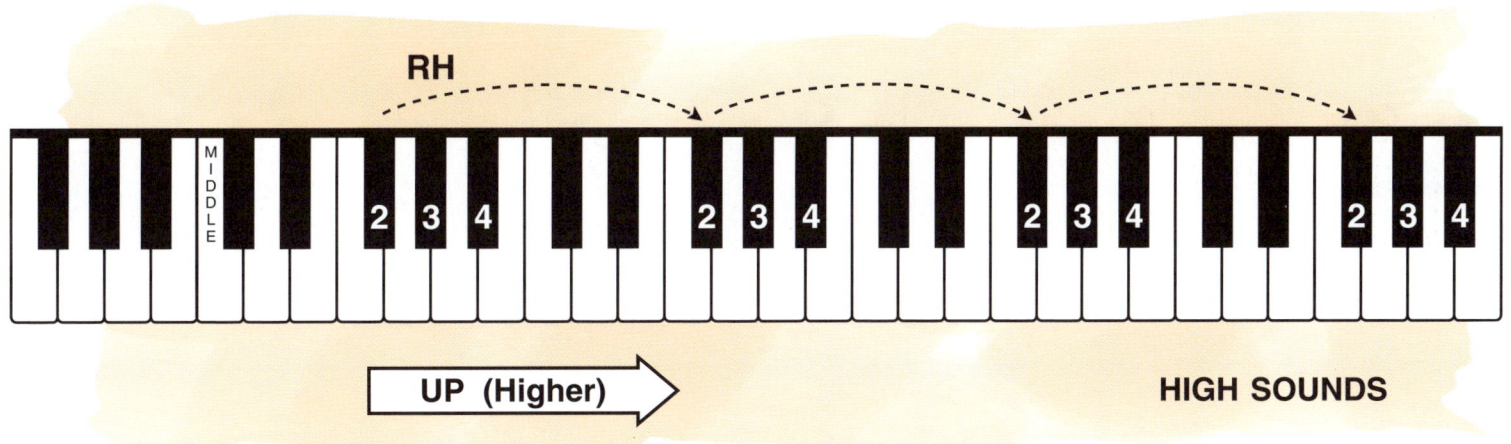

🔊 GM/CD 1-22 (66)

UNIT 2 MORE KEYBOARD BASICS

Rhythm Drills

Clap (or tap) the following rhythms, counting aloud.

GM/CD 1-23 (67)

a.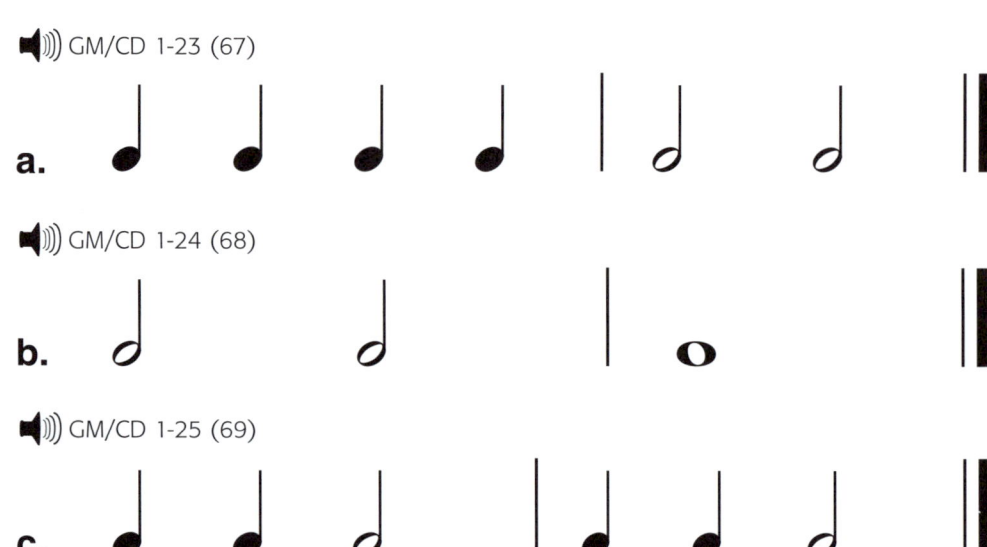

GM/CD 1-24 (68)

b.

GM/CD 1-25 (69)

c.

Composition / Improvisation

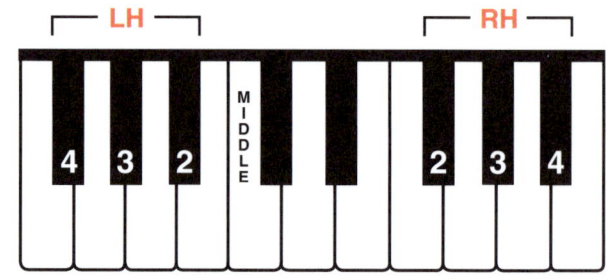

1. Create melodies in the given position using the rhythm pattern below. Begin and end each hand with the given finger numbers.

2. Write the finger number below each left hand note and above each right hand note for your favorite melody.

3. Write a different dynamic sign (f or p) in each box.

GM/CD 1-26 (70)

 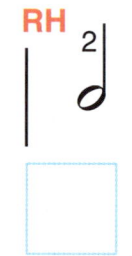   

Sight Reading

1. Clap (or tap) & count aloud.

2. Play finger numbers in the air & count.

3. Play & count.

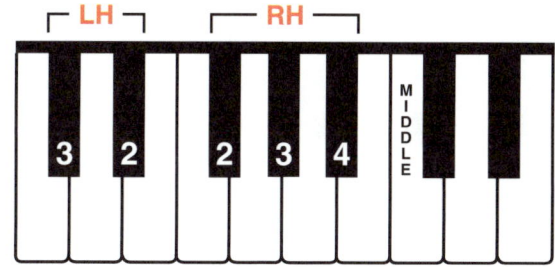

🔊 GM/CD 1-27 (71)

a.

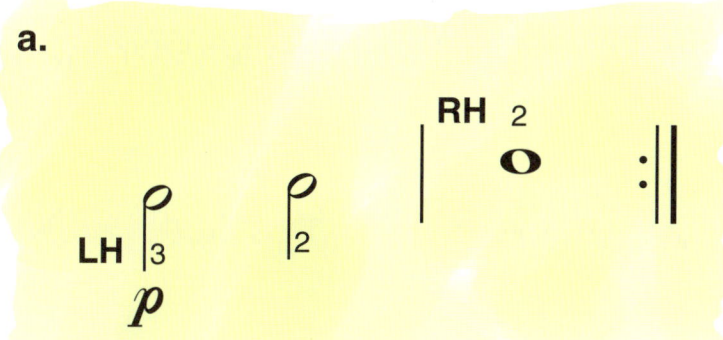

🔊 GM/CD 1-28 (72)

b.

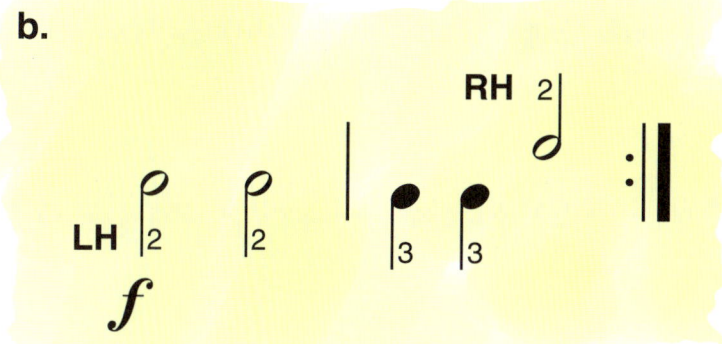

🔊 GM/CD 1-29 (73)

c.

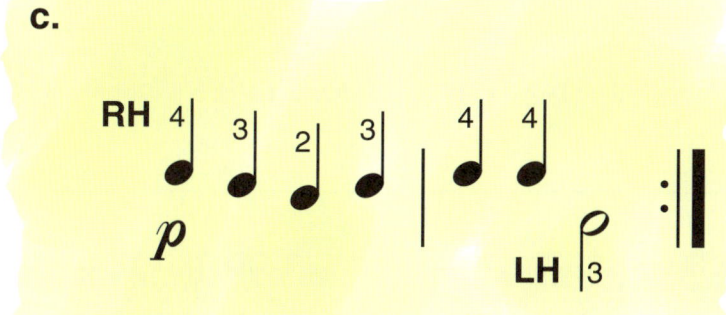

🔊 GM/CD 1-30 (74)

d.

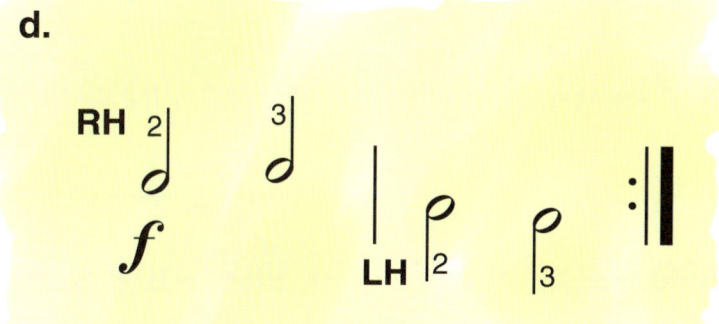

Jolly Old Saint Nicholas

FOR BLACK-KEY GROUPS BELOW MIDDLE

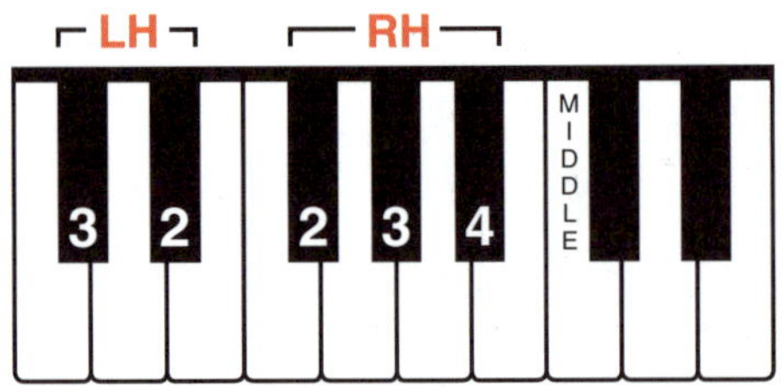

GM/CD 1-31 (75)

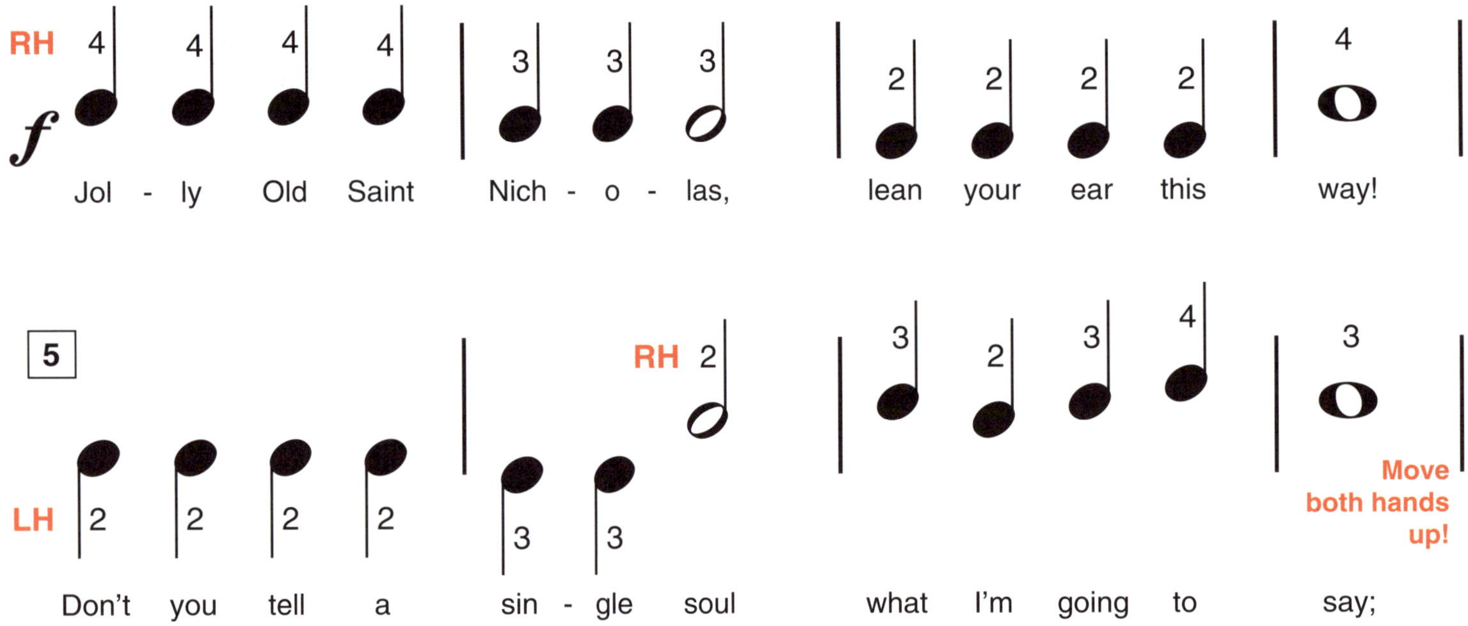

RH 4 4 4 4 | 3 3 3 | 2 2 2 2 | 4

Jol - ly Old Saint Nich - o - las, lean your ear this way!

5

LH 2 2 2 2 | 3 3 | **RH** 2 | 3 2 3 4 | 3

Don't you tell a sin - gle soul what I'm going to say;

Move both hands up!

DUET PART (Student plays on black-key groups ABOVE the middle of the keyboard.)

FOR BLACK-KEY GROUPS ABOVE MIDDLE

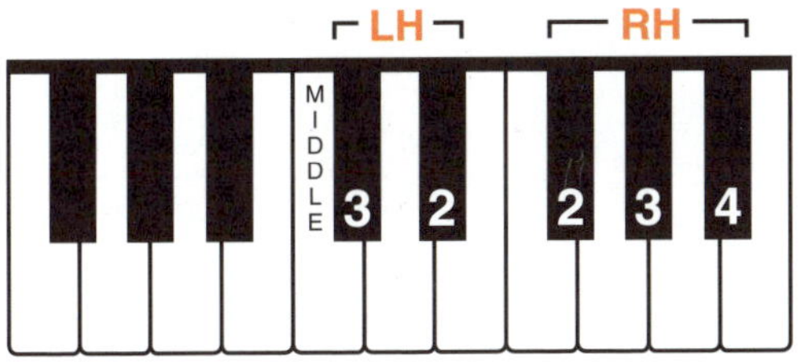

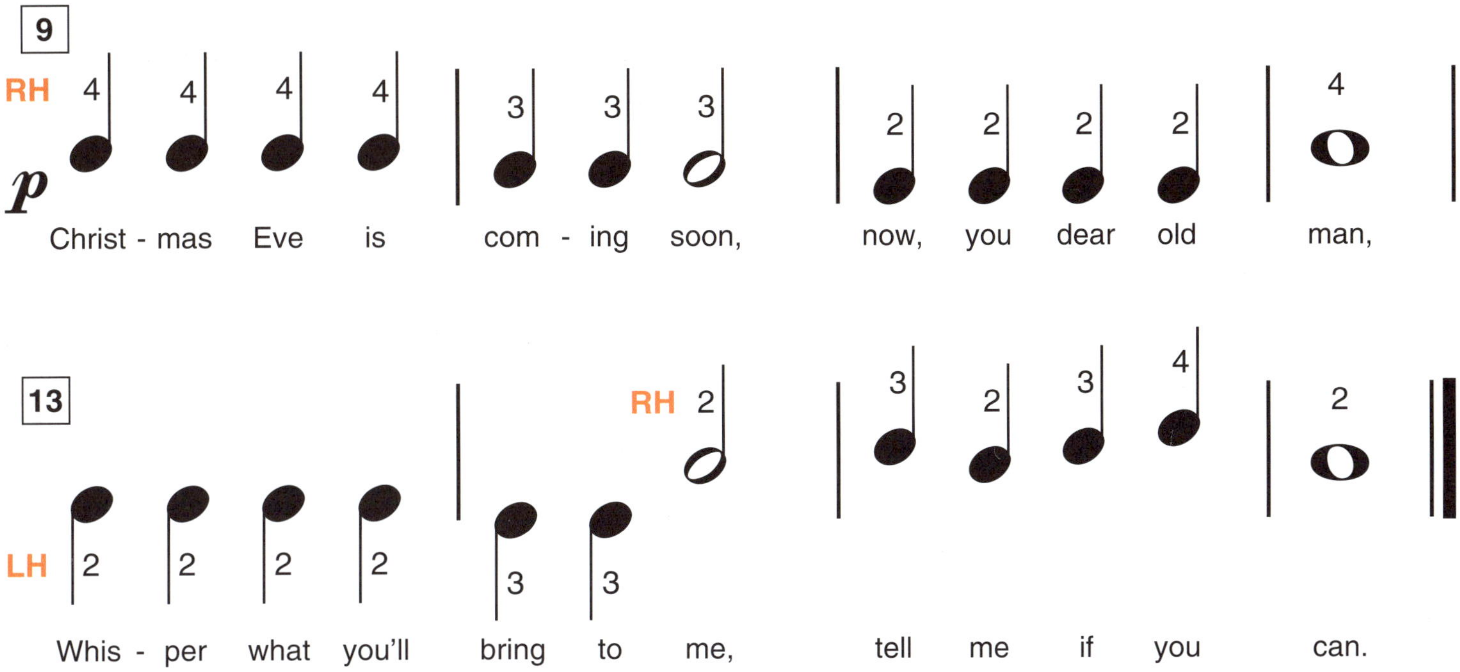

9

RH

p

4	4	4	4	3	3	3	2	2	2	2	4
Christ -	mas	Eve	is	com	- ing	soon,	now,	you	dear	old	man,

13

LH

2	2	2	2	3	3	RH 2	3	2	3	4	2
Whis -	per	what	you'll	bring	to	me,	tell	me	if	you	can.

UNIT 3 COMBINING 2- AND 3-BLACK-KEY GROUPS

Old MacDonald

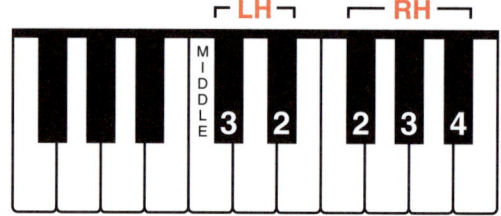

🔊 GM/CD 1-32 (76)

END HERE
after playing
the next page!

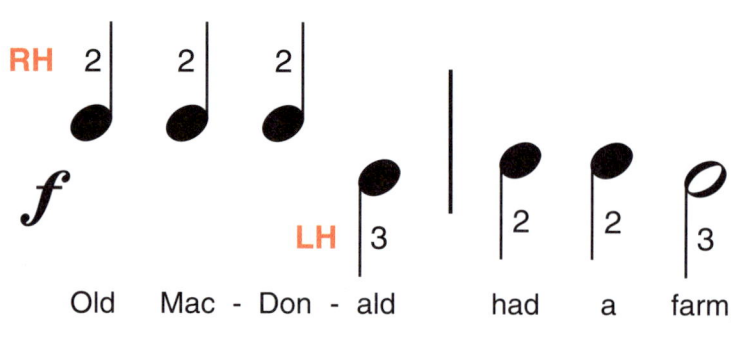

Old Mac - Don - ald   had   a   farm,   E - I - E - I - O!

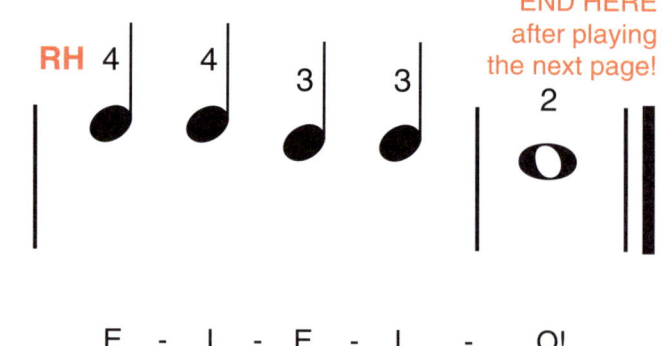

5

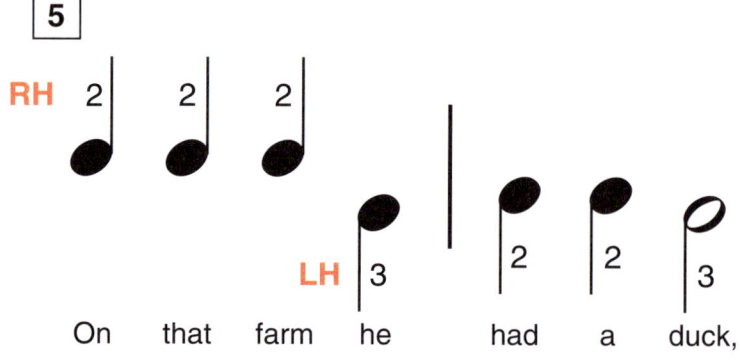

On   that   farm   he   had   a   duck,   E - I - E - I - O!

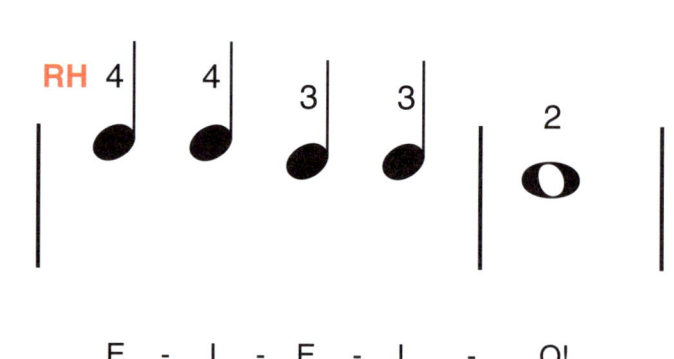

DUET PART

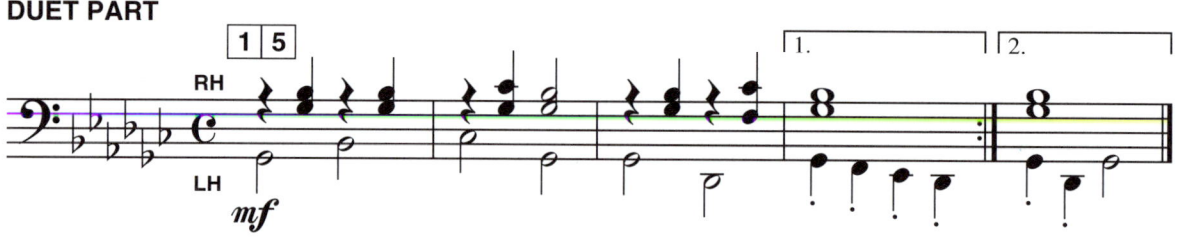

For the next page, rest 4 measures, then
repeat the above, taking the 2nd ending.

UNIT 3 COMBINING 2- AND 3-BLACK-KEY GROUPS

Sound Effects

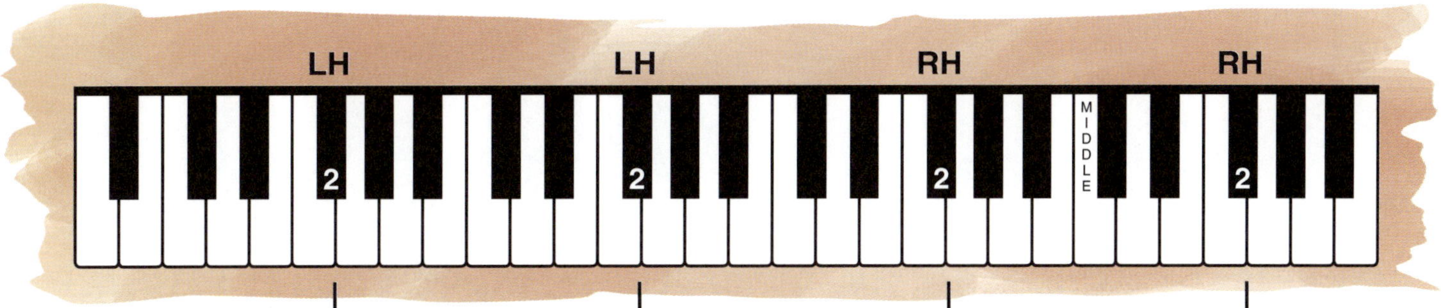

LH
LH
RH
RH
2
2
2
2
MIDDLE

Play LH 2 on bottom key of lowest 3 black key group on the keyboard.

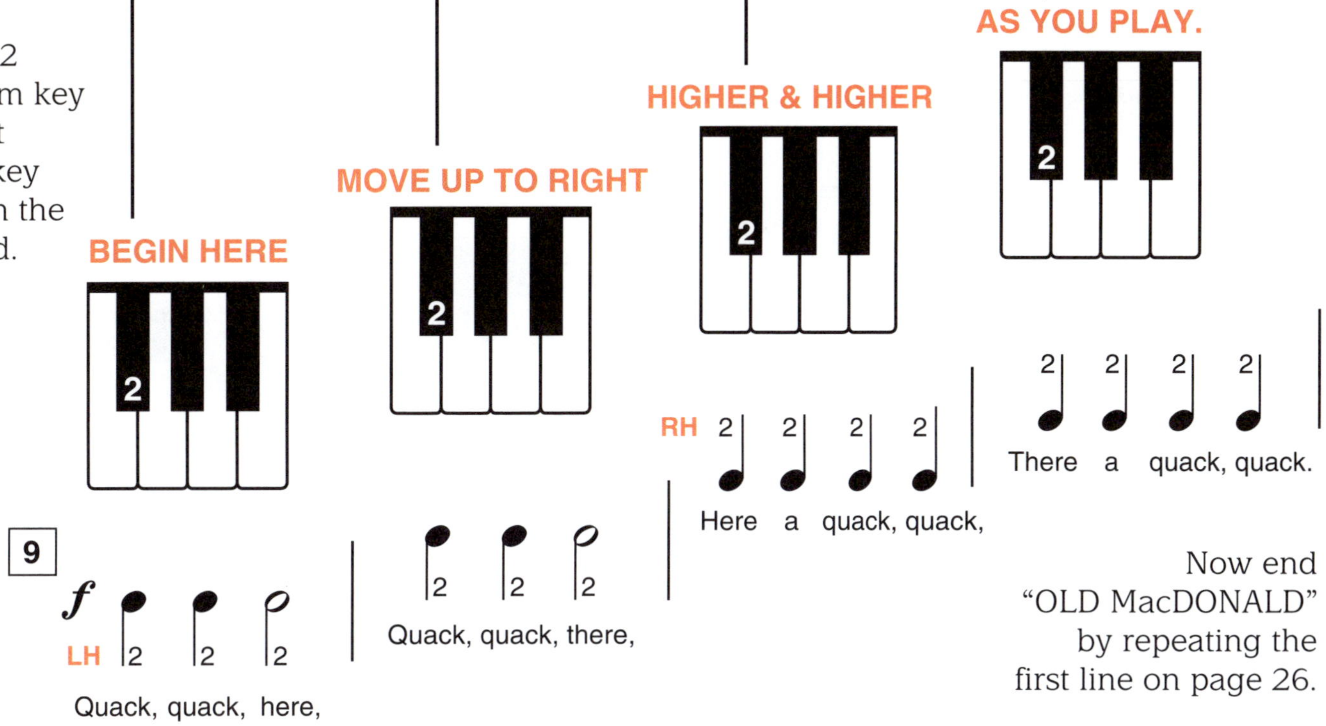

BEGIN HERE
MOVE UP TO RIGHT
HIGHER & HIGHER
AS YOU PLAY.
9
f
LH 2 2 2
Quack, quack, here,
2 2 2
Quack, quack, there,
RH 2 2 2 2
Here a quack, quack,
2 2 2 2
There a quack, quack.

Now end "OLD MacDONALD" by repeating the first line on page 26.

Play the entire song as many times as you like.
Use different animals: PIG ("oink, oink, here.")
COW ("moo, moo, here.")

Add as many animals as you wish to MacDonald's Farm.

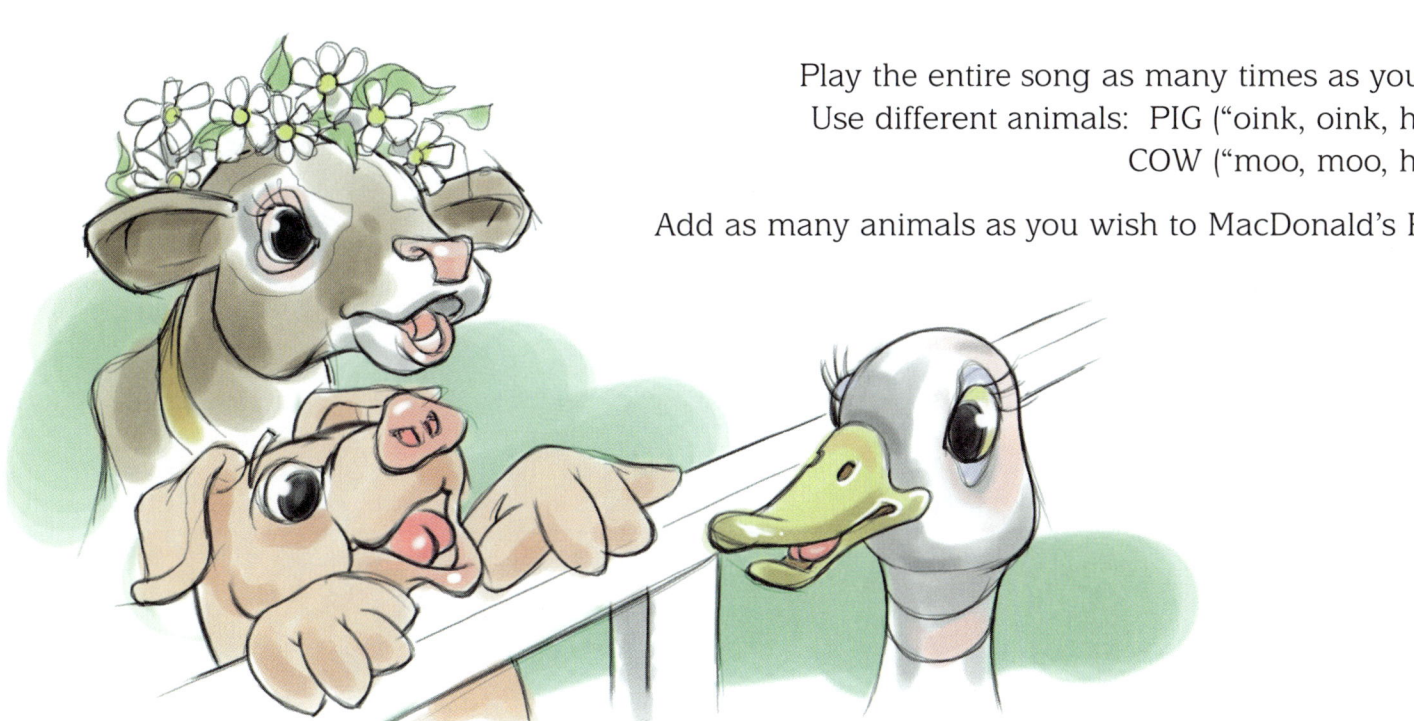

Ear Training

Rhythm Patterns

1. Your teacher will clap two rhythm patterns.

   - Circle SAME if the patterns are the SAME.

   - Circle DIFFERENT if the patterns are DIFFERENT.

2. Your teacher will clap a rhythm pattern.
   Circle the pattern that you hear.

🔊 GM/CD 1-33 (77)

1a SAME different

1b SAME different

1c SAME different

1d SAME different

🔊 GM/CD 1-34 (78)

2a

2b

2c

2d

TEACHER: See page 79.

Rhythm Drills

Clap (or tap) the following rhythms, counting aloud.

🔊 GM/CD 1-35 (79)

a.

🔊 GM/CD 1-36 (80)

b.

🔊 GM/CD 1-37 (81)

c.

Composition / Improvisation

1. Create melodies in the given position using the rhythm pattern below. Begin and end each hand with the given finger numbers.

2. Write the finger number below each left hand note and above each right hand note for your favorite melody.

3. Write a different dynamic sign (f or p) in each box.

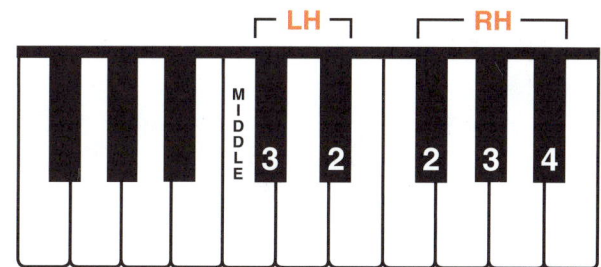

🔊 GM/CD 1-38 (82)

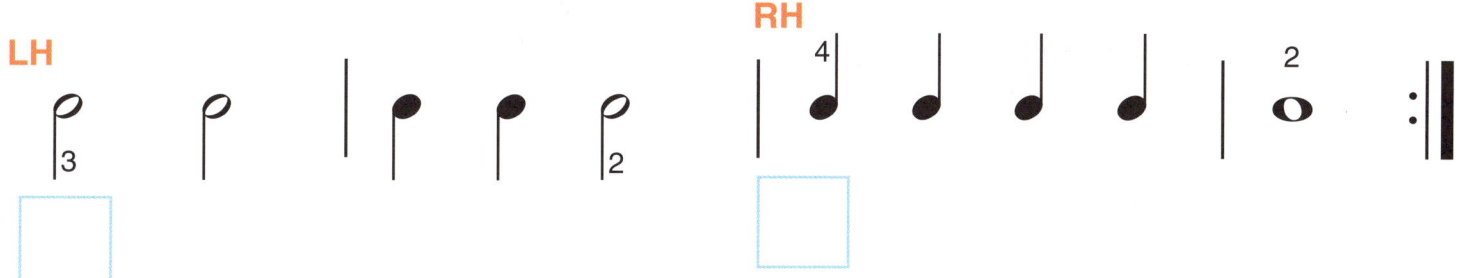

Sailor Jack

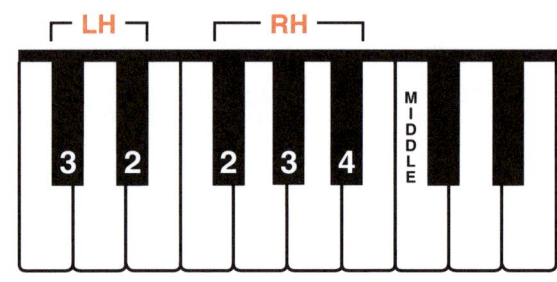

GM/CD 1-39 (83)

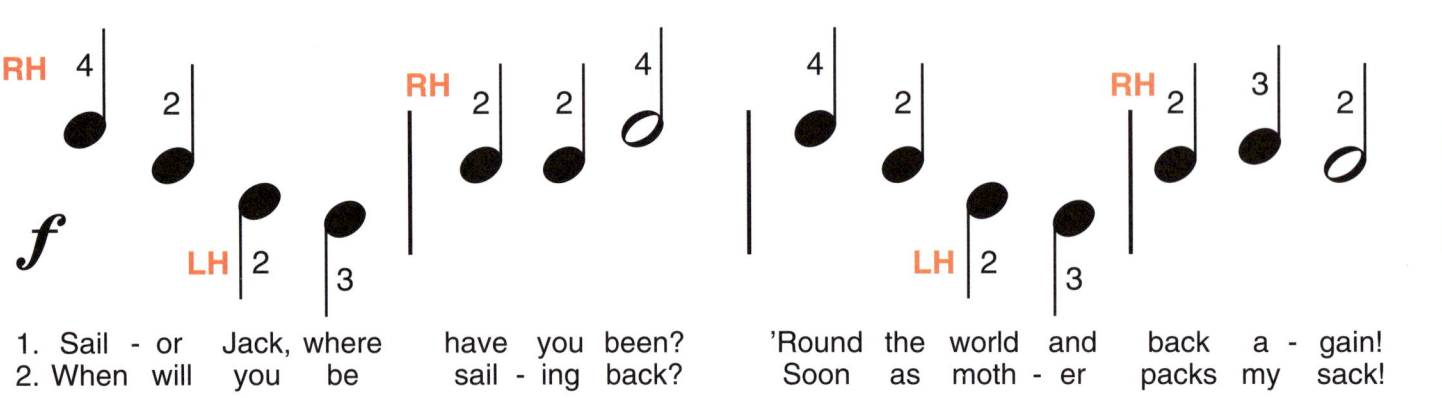

1. Sail - or   Jack, where   have   you   been?   'Round   the   world   and   back   a - gain!
2. When   will   you   be   sail - ing   back?   Soon   as   moth - er   packs   my   sack!

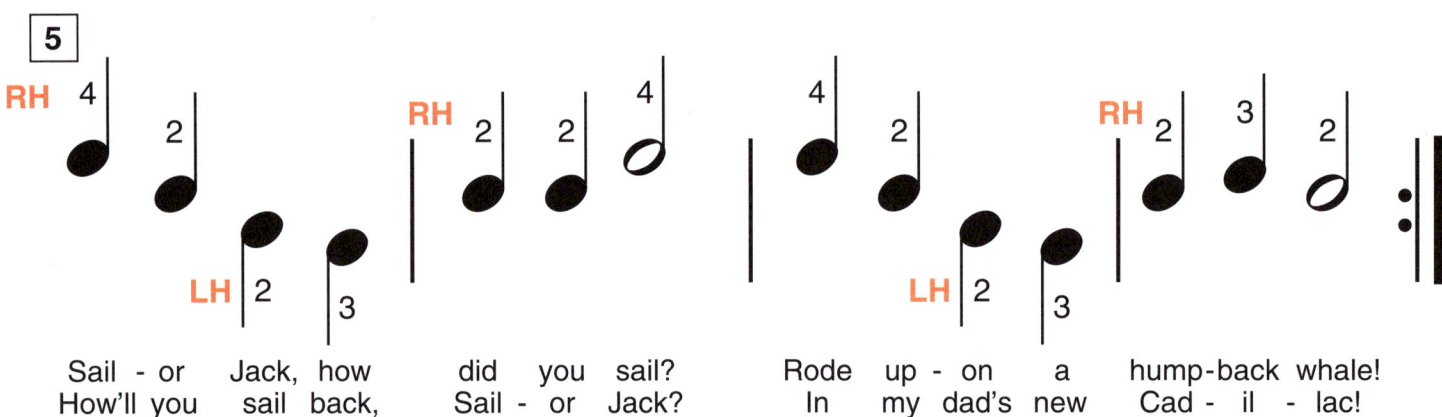

Sail - or   Jack, how   did   you   sail?   Rode   up - on   a   hump-back whale!
How'll you   sail back,   Sail - or   Jack?   In   my   dad's   new   Cad - il - lac!

TEACHER: See page 76.

Sailor Jack

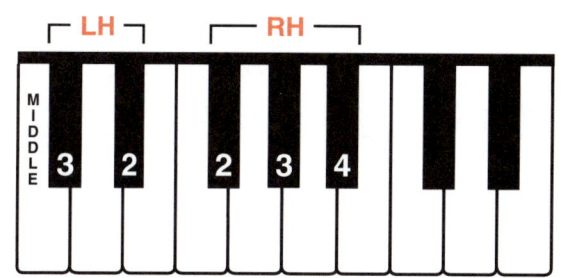

 GM/CD 1-39 (83)

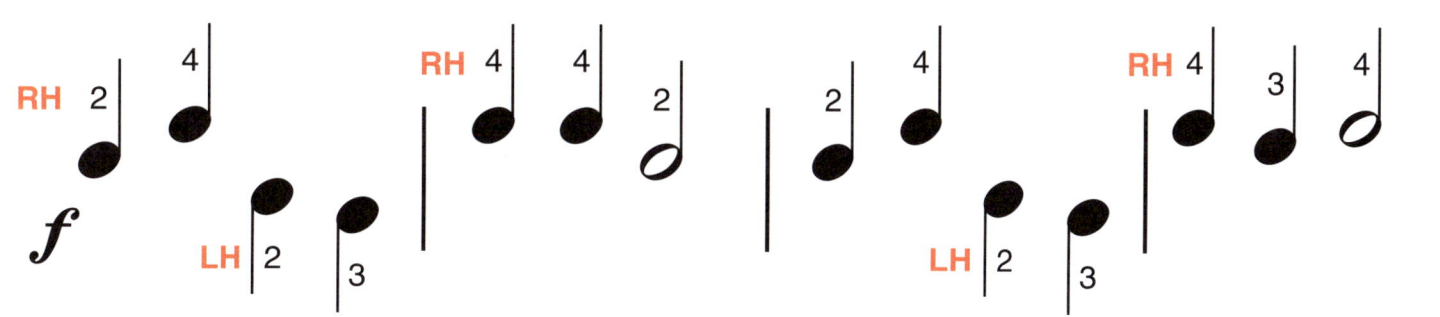

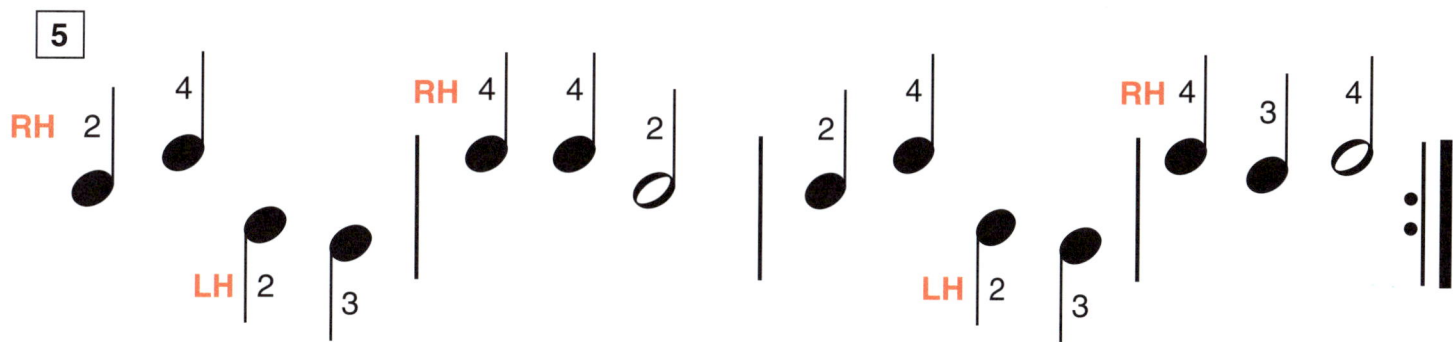

TEACHER: See page 76.

Sailor Jack

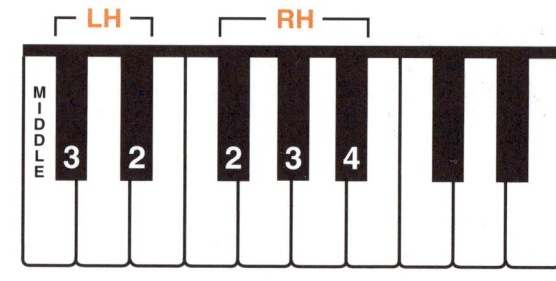

(Both hands 1 octave higher than shown throughout)

🔊 GM/CD 1-39 (83)

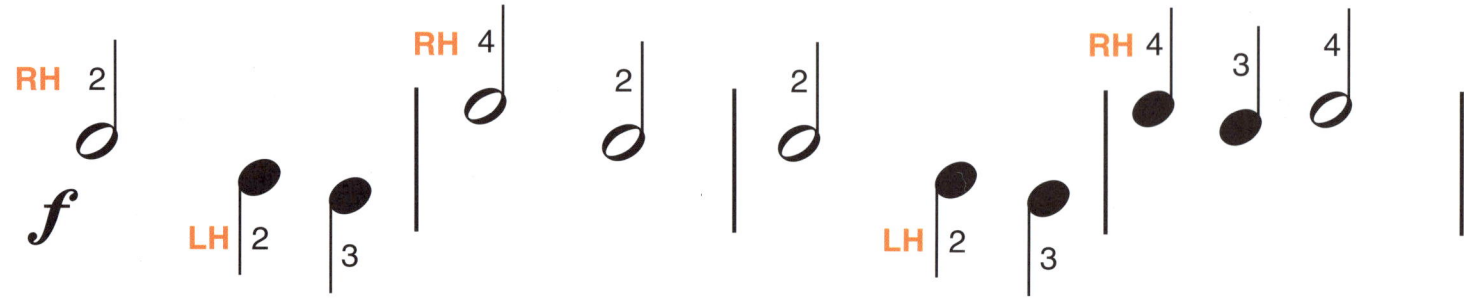

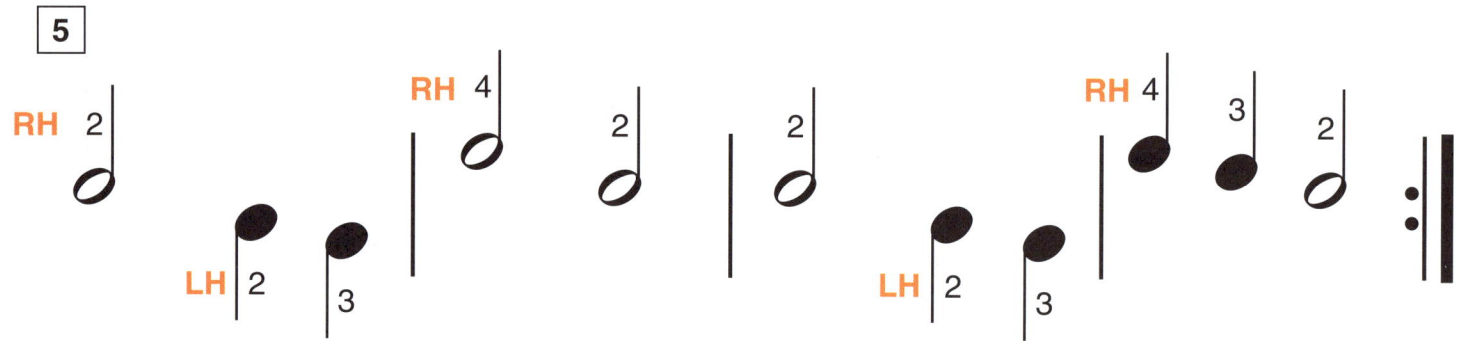

TEACHER: See page 76.

Ensemble PART 4

Sailor Jack

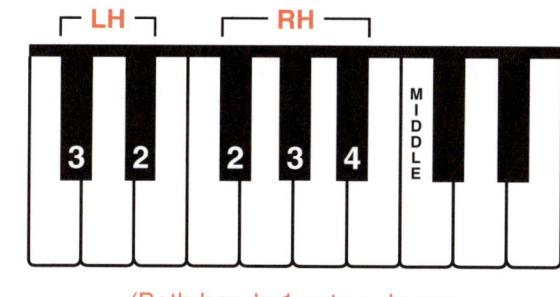

(Both hands 1 octave lower than shown throughout)

🔊 GM/CD 1-39 (83)

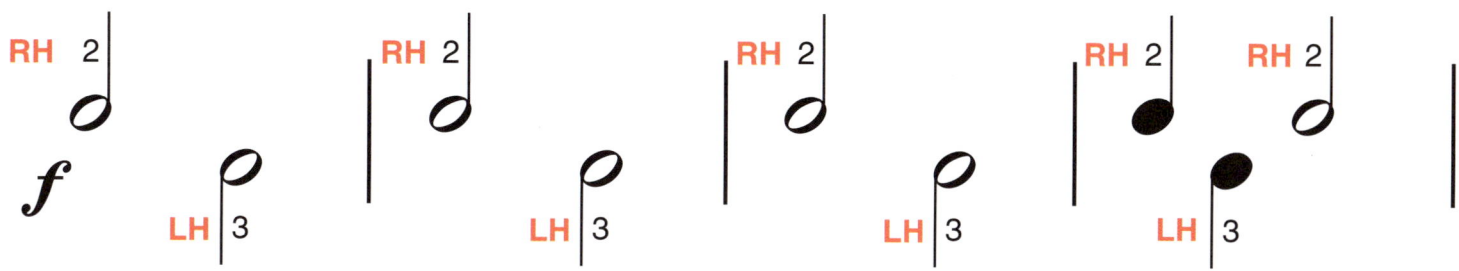

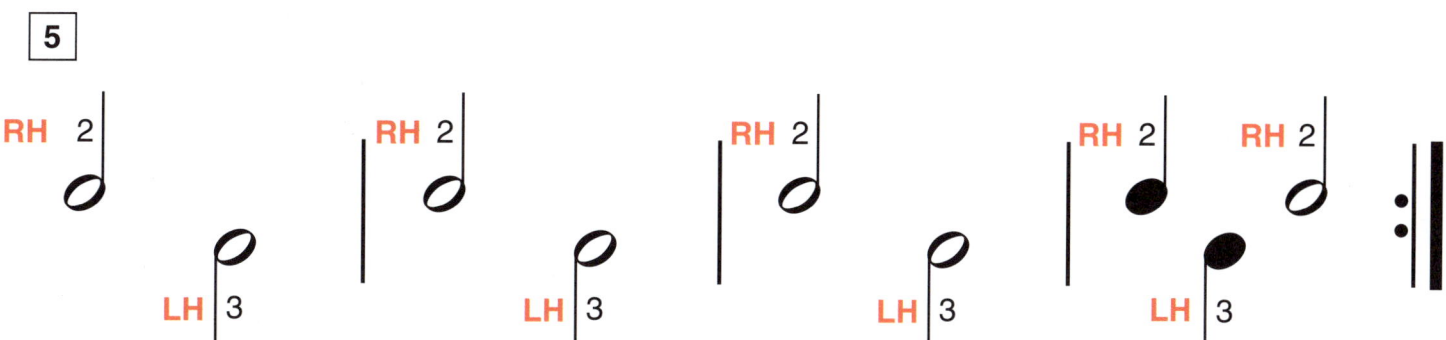

TEACHER: See page 76.

UNIT 3 COMBINING 2- AND 3-BLACK-KEY GROUPS

A   B   C   D   E   F   G

1. Piano keys are named for the first seven letters of the alphabet. The key names are A B C D E F G, used over and over!

2. The lowest key on the piano is A. Find the lowest A on your keyboard.

3. The C nearest the middle of the piano (under the brand name) is called MIDDLE C. Find MIDDLE C on your keyboard.

4. The highest key on the piano is C. Find the highest C on your keyboard.

5. Going up the keyboard, the notes sound higher and higher. While most acoustic pianos have 88 keys, some digital keyboards may have fewer.

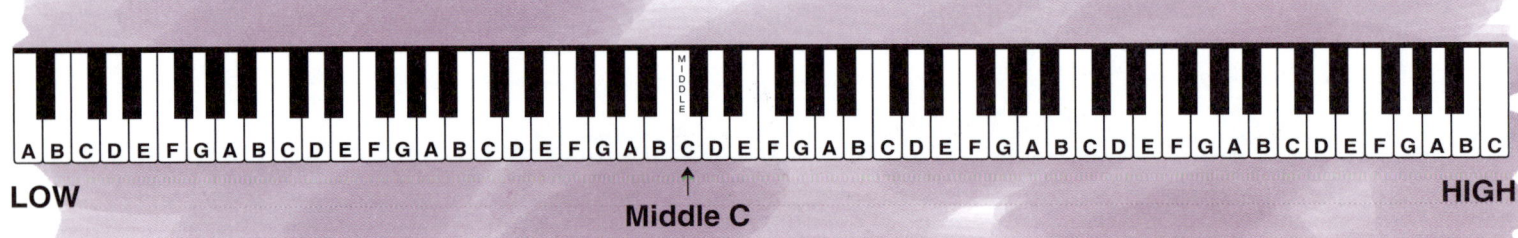

A B C D E F G A B C D E F G A B C D E F G A B C D E F G A B C D E F G A B C D E F G A B C D E F G A B C

LOW   ↑ Middle C   **HIGH**

Beginning at the low end and moving UP the keyboard, play and name
every white key beginning with the bottom A, using the indicated rhythm.

- Use LH 3 for keys below the middle
  of the keyboard.

- Use RH 3 for keys above the middle
  of the keyboard.

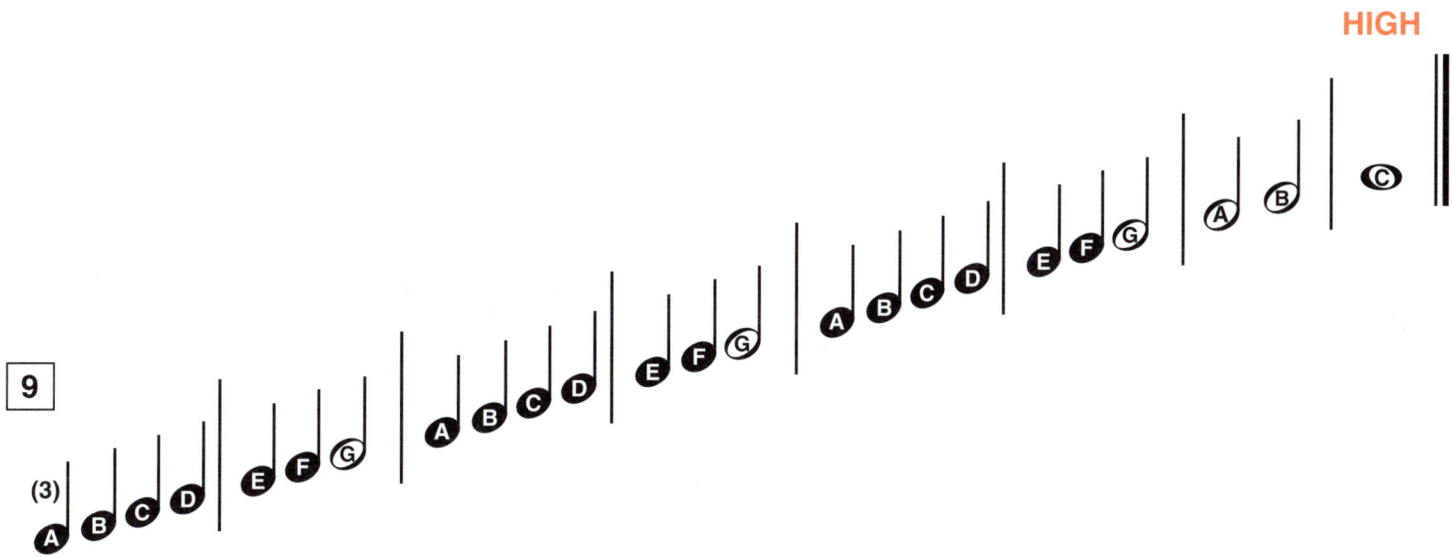

🔊))) GM/CD 1-40 (84)

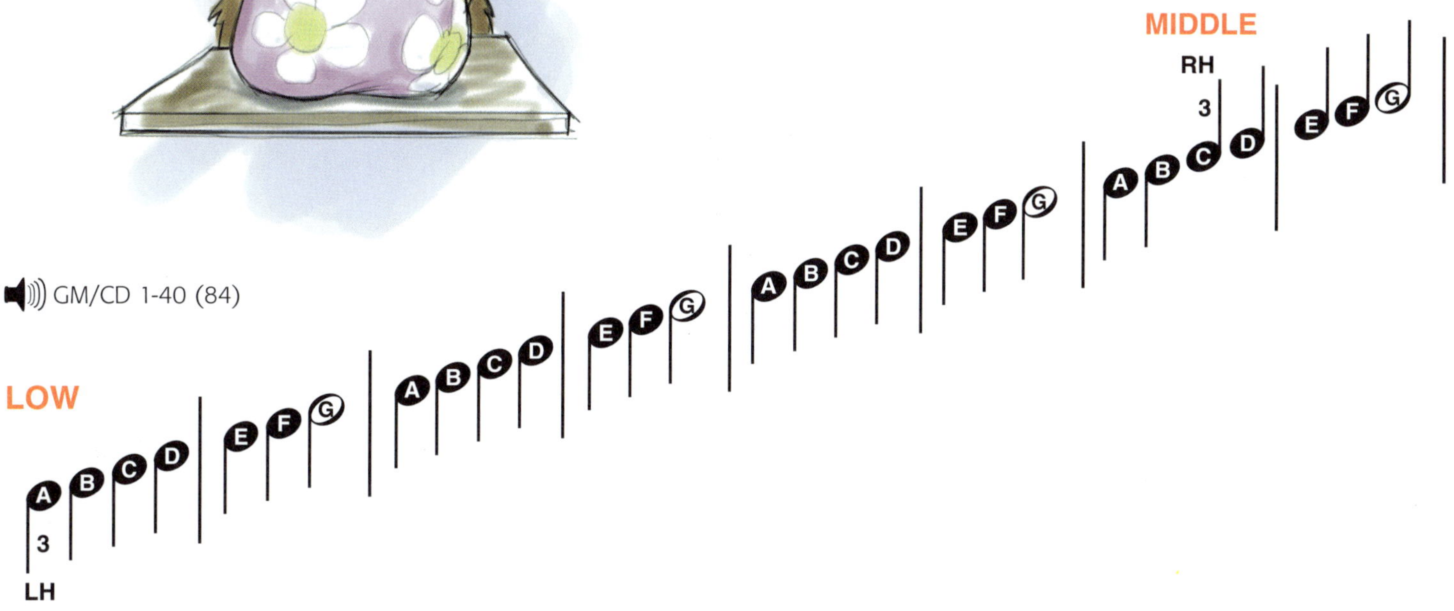

UNIT 4 NAMING WHITE KEYS

An Easy Way to Find Any White Key

Use LH 3 for keys below the middle of the keyboard.

Use RH 3 for keys above the middle of the keyboard.

1. Play all the A's on your piano.

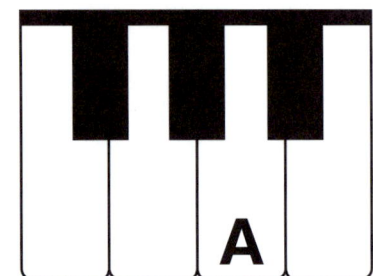

A

2. Play all the B's.

B

3. Play all the C's.

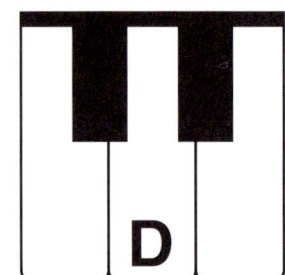

C

4. Play all the D's.

D

5. Play all the E's.

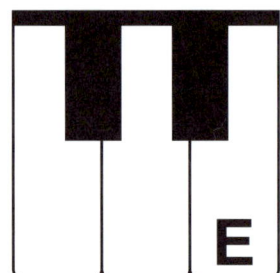

E

6. Play all the F's.

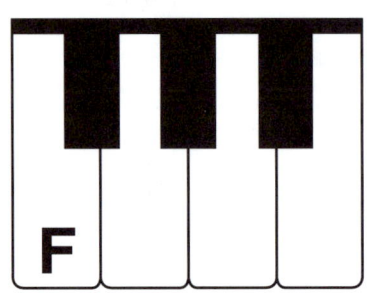

F

7. Play all the G's.

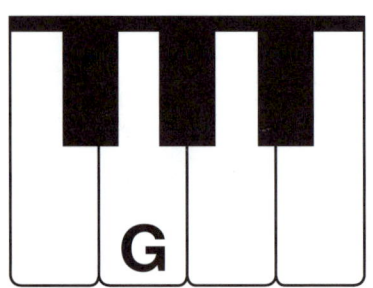

G

 Theory

White Keys

Piano keys are named for the first seven letters of the alphabet.

A B C D E F G

1. Write the missing letter names from the music alphabet on each line.

    - **A** ___ **C** ___ **E** ___ **G**
    - ___ **B** ___ **D** ___ **F** ___
    - **A** ___ ___ **D** ___ ___ ___

2. Write the MUSICAL ALPHABET in the squares on this keyboard. Begin with A.

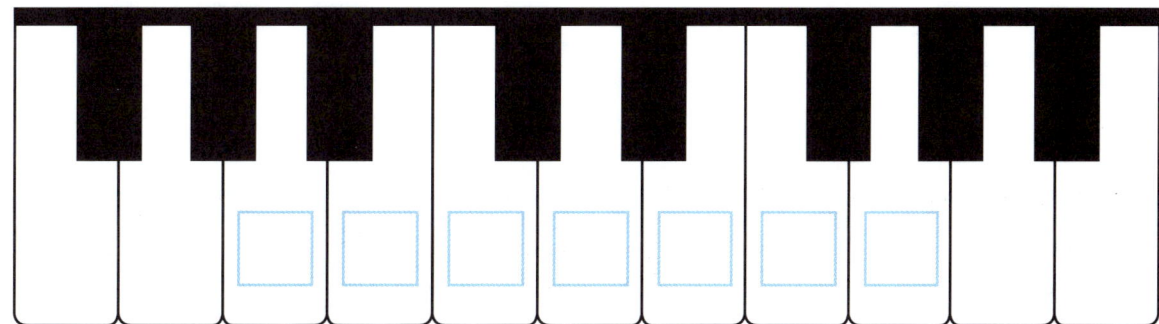

A is between the
   2nd & 3rd keys
   of any
   3-black-key group!

3. Find all the A's on this keyboard. Print an A on each one.

UNIT 4 NAMING WHITE KEYS

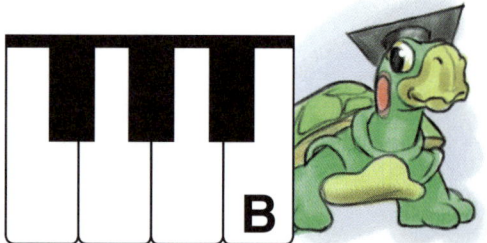

B is on the RIGHT
of any
3-black-key group!

4. Find all the B's on this keyboard. Print a B on each one.

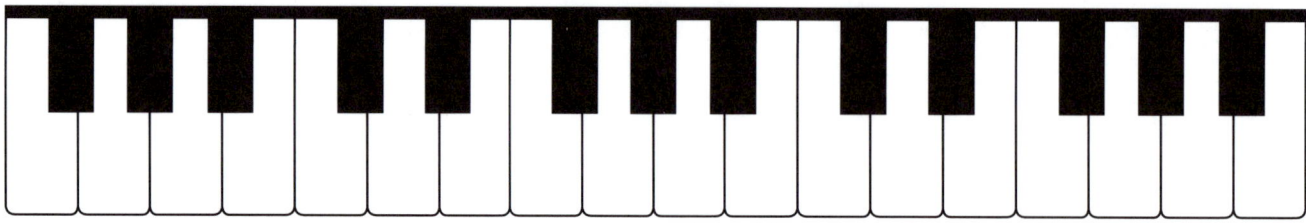

C is on the LEFT
of any
2-black-key group!

5. Find all the C's on this keyboard. Print a C on each one.

D is in the MIDDLE
of any
2-black-key group!

6. Find all the D's on this keyboard. Print a D on each one.

E is on the RIGHT
of any
2-black-key group!

7. Find all the E's on this keyboard. Print an E on each one.

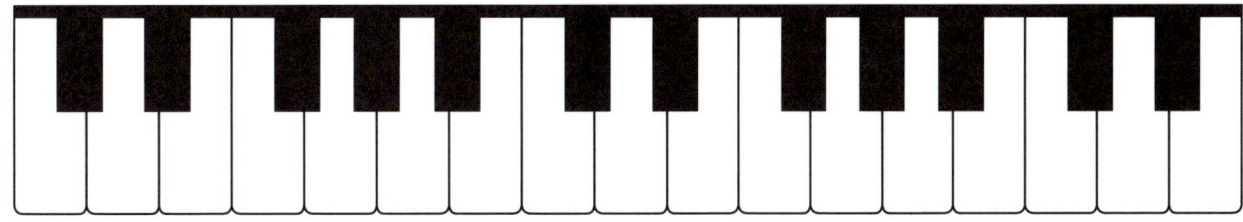

F is on the LEFT
of any
3-black-key group!

8. Find all the F's on this keyboard. Print an F on each one.

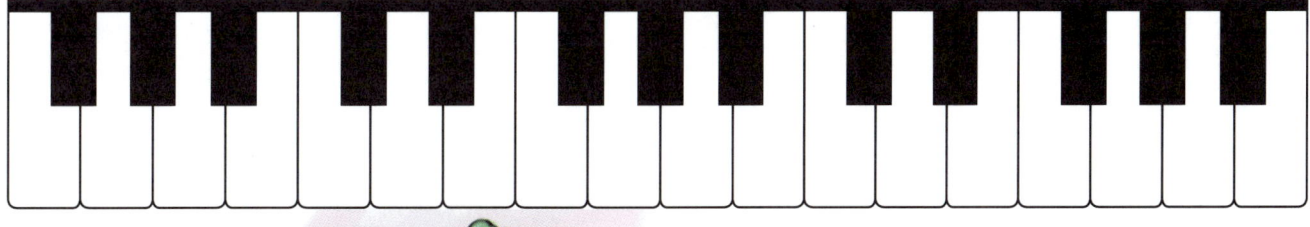

G is between the
1st & 2nd keys
of any
3-black-key group!

9. Find all the G's on this keyboard. Print a G on each one.

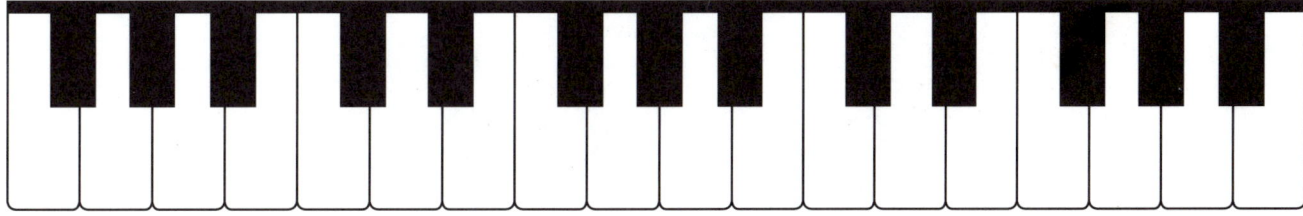

NOTE: You are now ready to play the game **Musical Adventures** (*Keys on the Keyboard* game cards)!

Technique

With LH 1 2 3, begin on the E above middle C and play all of the E-D-C groups going DOWN the keyboard, using the indicated rhythm and finger numbers. Use the keyboard diagram as an aid to moving down the keyboard.

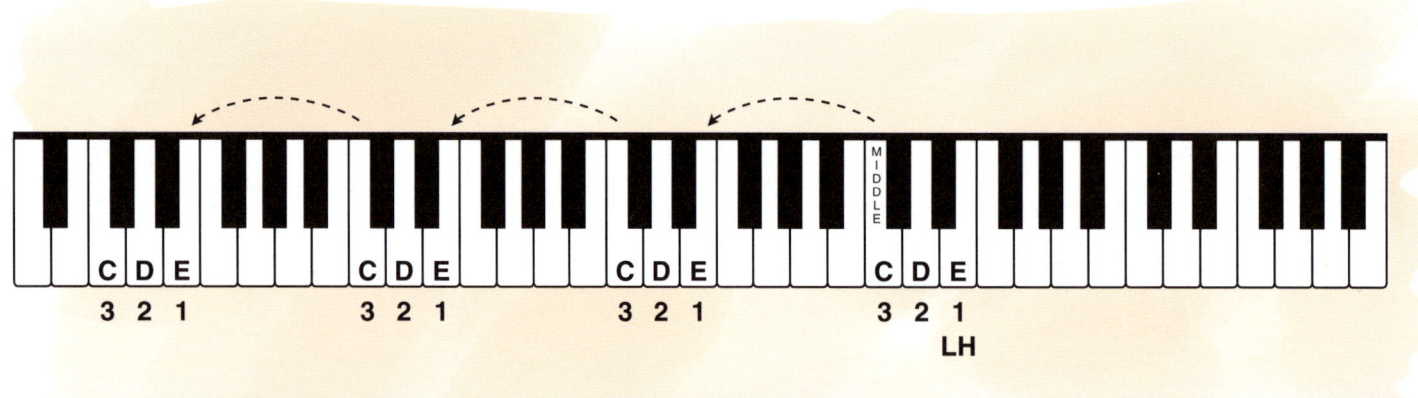

🔊 GM/CD 1-41 (85)

With RH 1 2 3, begin on middle C and play all of the C-D-E groups going UP the keyboard, using the indicated rhythm and finger numbers. Use the keyboard diagram as an aid to moving up the keyboard.

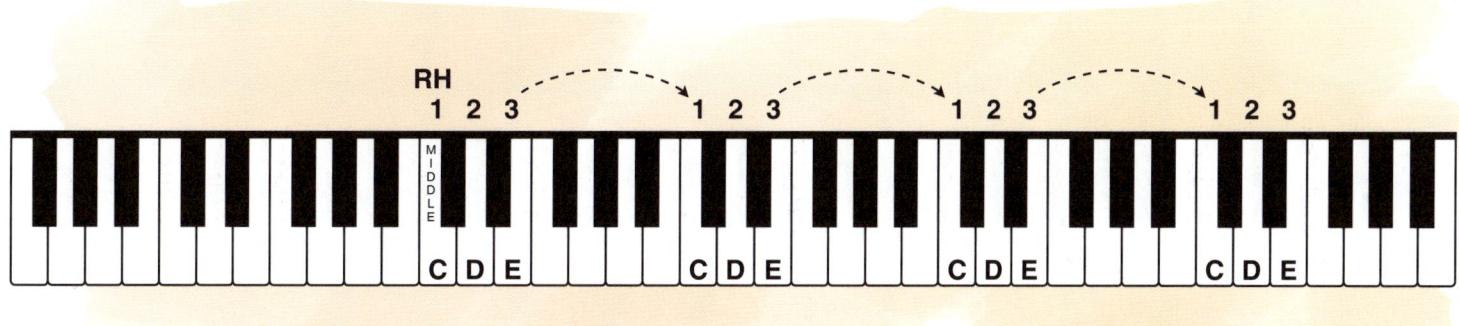

🔊 GM/CD 1-42 (86)

UNIT 4 NAMING WHITE KEYS

With LH 1 2 3 4, begin on the B below middle C and play all of the B-A-G-F groups going DOWN the keyboard, using the indicated rhythm and finger numbers. Use the keyboard diagram as an aid to moving down the keyboard.

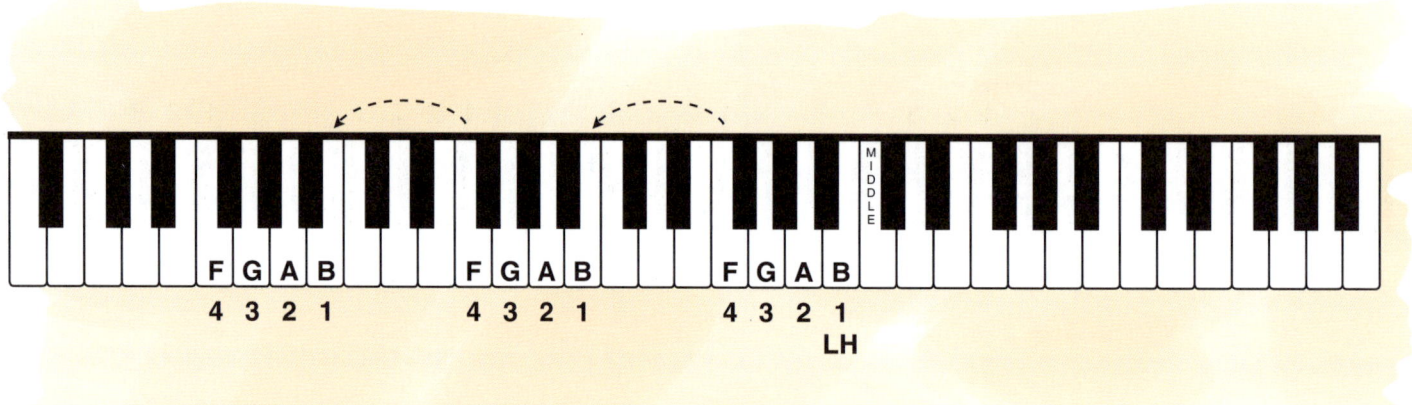

GM/CD 1-43 (87)

With RH 1 2 3 4, begin on the F above middle C and play all of the F-G-A-B groups going UP the keyboard, using the indicated rhythm and finger numbers. Use the keyboard diagram as an aid to moving up the keyboard.

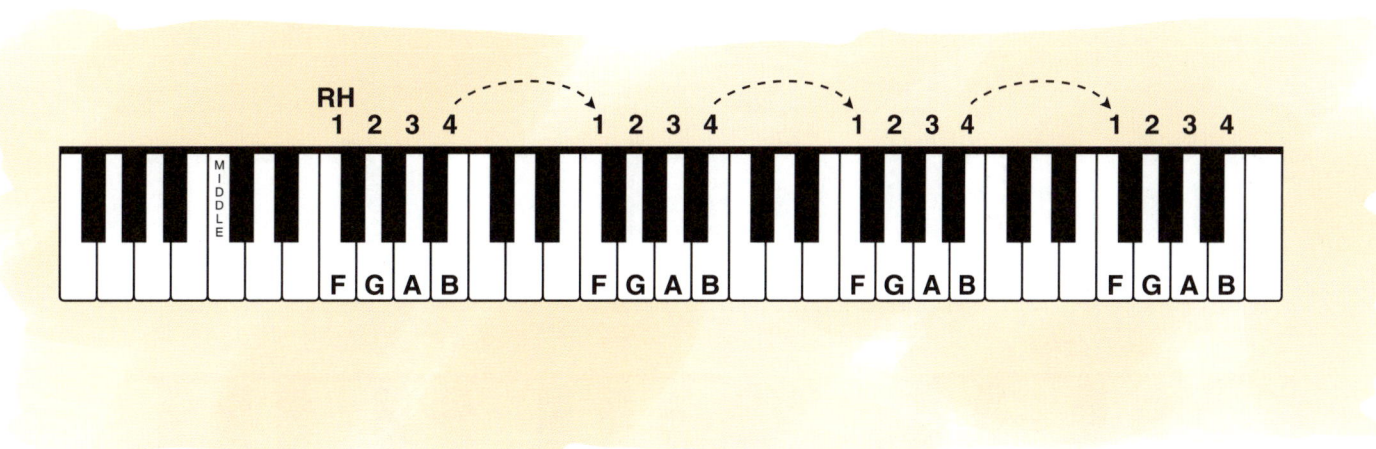

GM/CD 1-44 (88)

UNIT 4 NAMING WHITE KEYS

Theory

Spelling Games

Write the letter name on each key marked X.
Each keyboard will spell a familiar word!

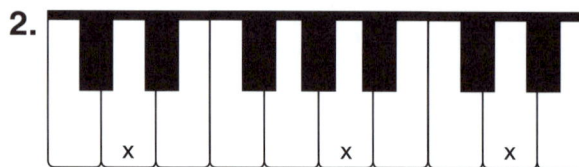

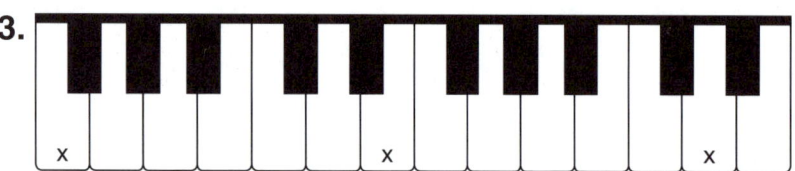

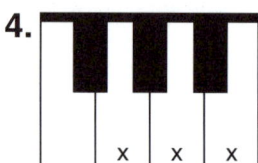

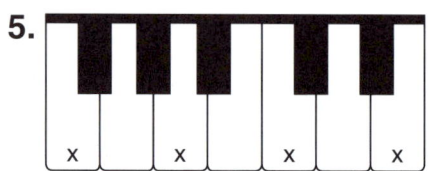

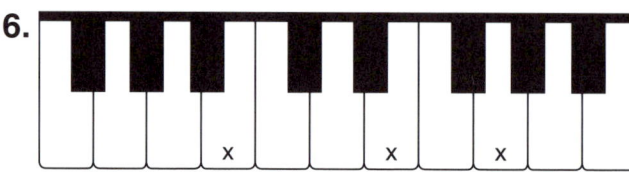

Spell BEAD on this keyboard.
Begin on the lowest B and use a higher key for each letter.

Spell ADD on this keyboard.
Begin on the lowest A and use a higher key for each letter.

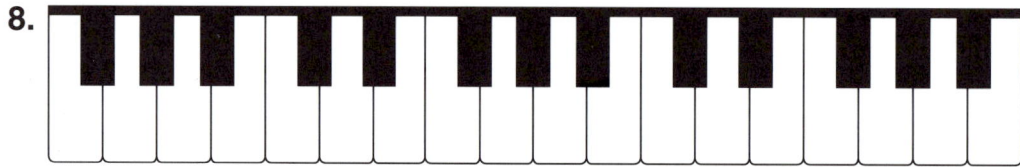

Spell CAGE on this keyboard.
Begin on the lowest C and use a higher key for each letter.

Batter Up!

1. Clap (or tap) & count.

2. Play & count.

3. Play & say note names.

4. Play & sing the words.

Follow these steps for each new piece.

The C nearest the middle of the keyboard is called "Middle C."

MIDDLE C POSITION

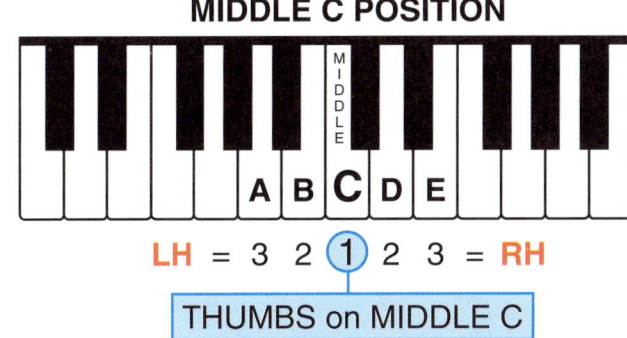

GM/CD 2-1 (42)

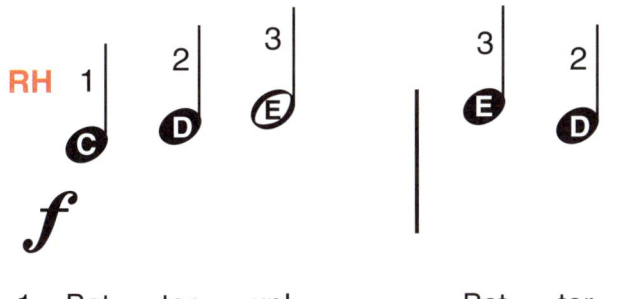

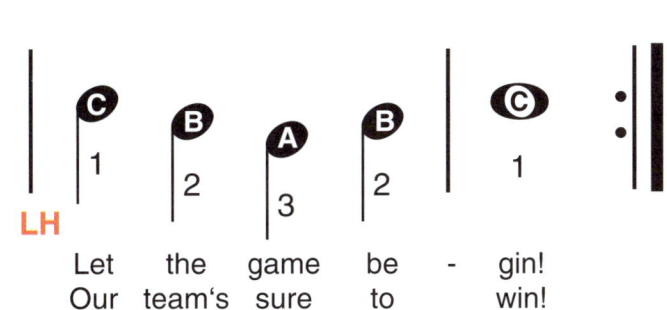

1. Bat - ter up! Bat - ter up! Let the game be - gin!
2. Bat - ter up! Bat - ter up! Our team's sure to win!

DUET PART

Sight Reading

1. Clap (or tap) & count.
2. Play finger numbers in the air & count.
3. Play & count.
4. Play & say note names.

MIDDLE C POSITION

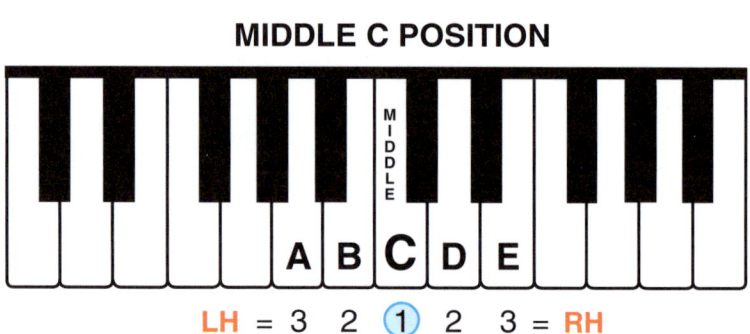

LH = 3   2   ①   2   3 = RH

🔊 GM/CD 2-2 (43)

a.

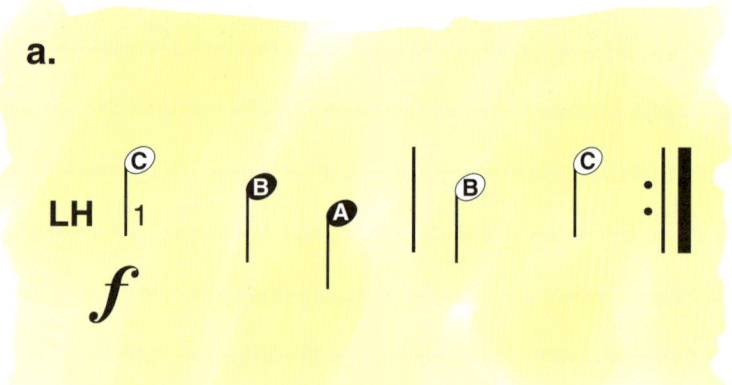

🔊 GM/CD 2-3 (44)

b.

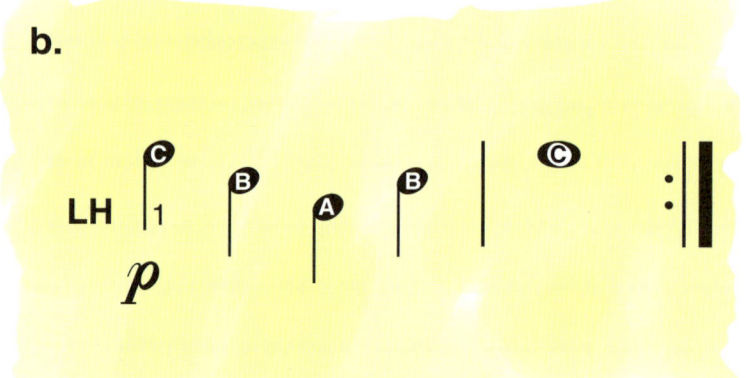

🔊 GM/CD 2-4 (45)

c.

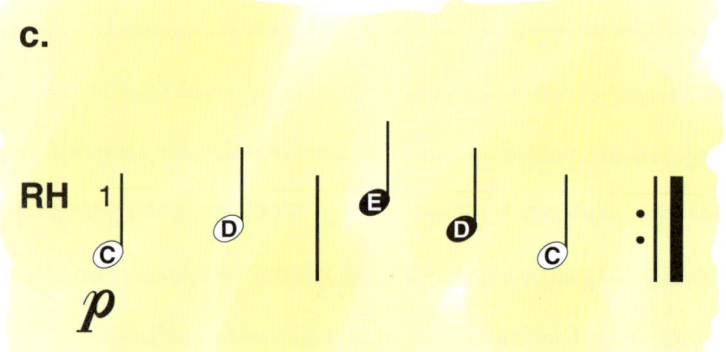

🔊 GM/CD 2-5 (46)

d.

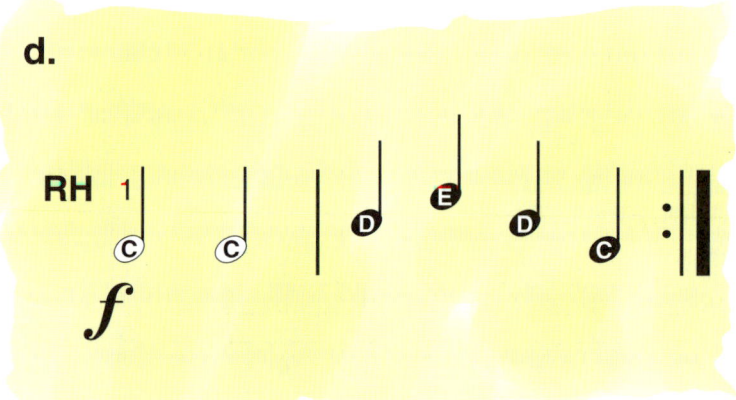

Music has numbers at the beginning called the **TIME SIGNATURE**.

$\frac{4}{4}$ means **4** beats to each measure.
a **quarter note** ♩ gets one beat.

1. Clap (or tap) the following rhythm.
2. Clap **ONCE** for each note, counting aloud as you clap.

COUNT: "1,   1,   1 - 2,   1 - 2 - 3 - 4"
OR: "1,   2,   3 - 4,   1 - 2 - 3 - 4"

My Clever Pup

MIDDLE C POSITION

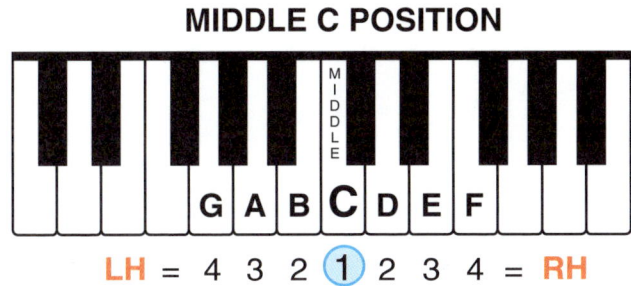

LH = 4 3 2 ① 2 3 4 = RH

🔊))) GM/CD 2-6 (47)

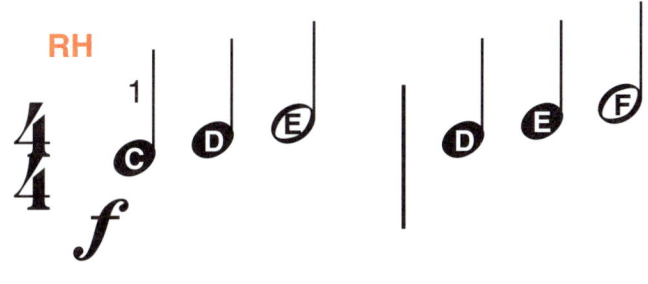 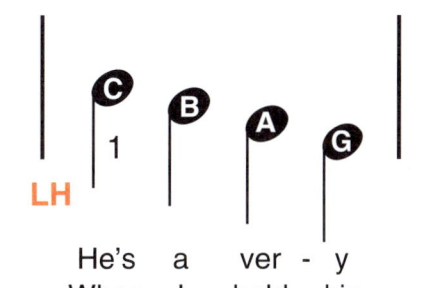 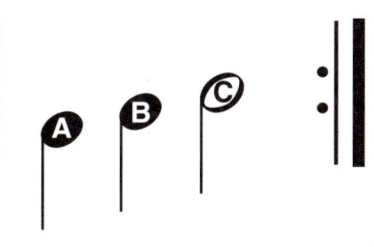

1. My dog's fun!   My dog's neat!   He's a   ver - y   clev - er pup!
2. He stands on   his front feet,   When I hold his   hind legs up!

DUET PART (Student plays 1 octave higher.)

Rhythm Drills

Clap (or tap) the following rhythms, counting aloud.

GM/CD 2-7 (48)

a.

GM/CD 2-8 (49)

b.

GM/CD 2-9 (50)

c.

Composition / Improvisation

MIDDLE C POSITION

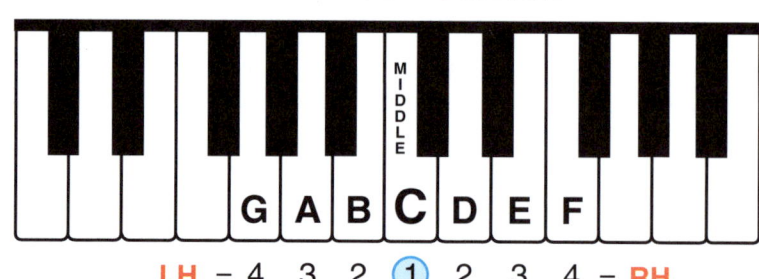

1. Create melodies in the given position using the rhythm pattern below.

2. Write the finger number above each right hand note and below each left hand note for your favorite melody.

3. Write the note name on the line below each note for your favorite melody.

4. Write a different dynamic sign (f or p) in each box.

GM/CD 2-10 (51)

 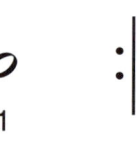

C __ __ __ E   G __ __ __ C

Ear Training

Middle C Position

Your teacher will play patterns that go UP or DOWN in the MIDDLE C POSITION. Circle the pattern that you hear.

🔊 GM/CD 2-11 (52)

a. C D (E)   E D (C)

b. C D (E)   E D (C)

c. (A) B (C)   C B (A)

d. (A) B (C)   C B (A)

e. G A B C   C B A G

f. G A B C   C B A G

g. C D E F   F E D C

h. C D E F   F E D C

TEACHER: See page 80.

The $\frac{4}{4}$ Time Signature

Music has numbers at the beginning called the **TIME SIGNATURE.**

The **TOP NUMBER** tells the number of beats in each measure.

The **BOTTOM NUMBER** tells the kind of note that gets ONE beat.

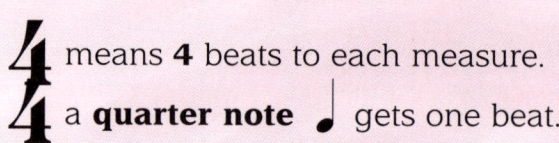

$\frac{4}{4}$ means **4** beats to each measure. a **quarter note** ♩ gets one beat.

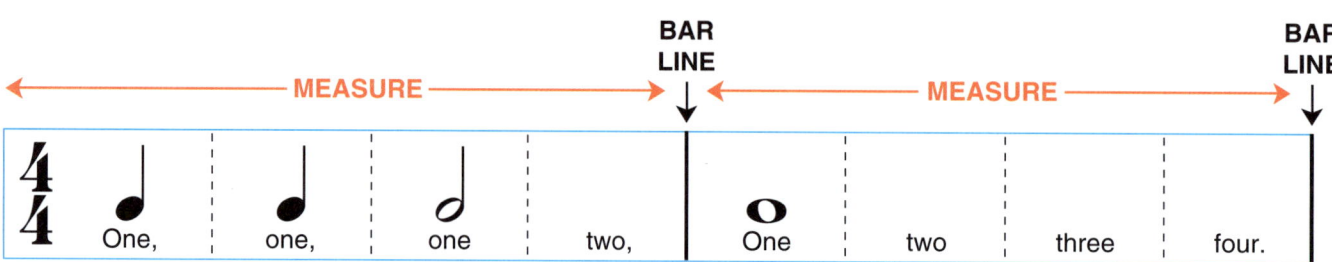

The notes in each measure must add up to **4 COUNTS!**

1. How many **QUARTER NOTES** can you have in each measure of $\frac{4}{4}$ time? _____
   Fill these measures with **QUARTER NOTES** with stems UP.

2. How many **HALF NOTES** can you have in each measure of $\frac{4}{4}$ time? _____
   Fill these measures with **HALF NOTES** with stems DOWN.

3. How many **WHOLE NOTES** can you have in each measure of $\frac{4}{4}$ time? _____
   Fill each measure with a **WHOLE NOTE.**

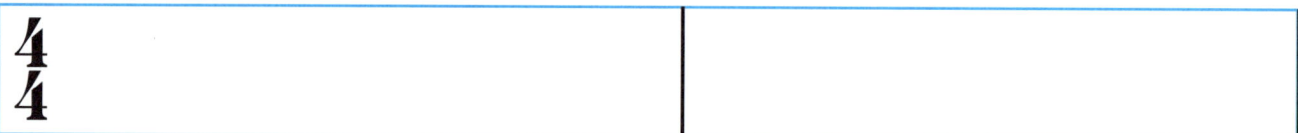

4. Add only **ONE NOTE** to each measure to make it complete.

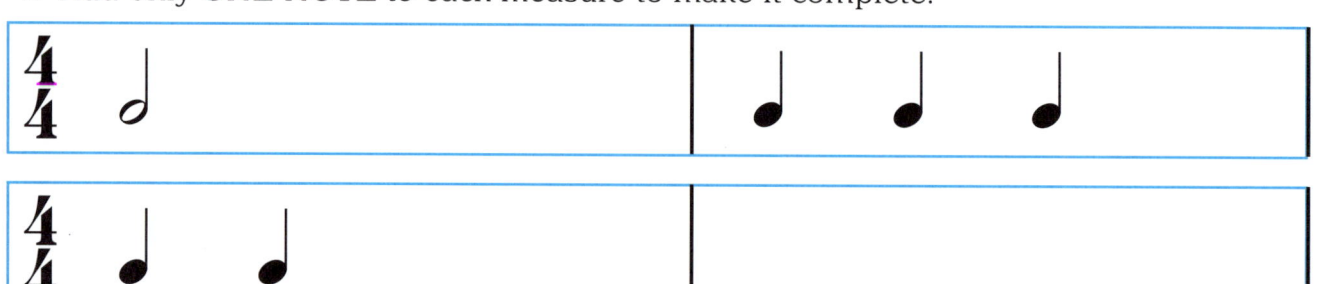

The Zoo

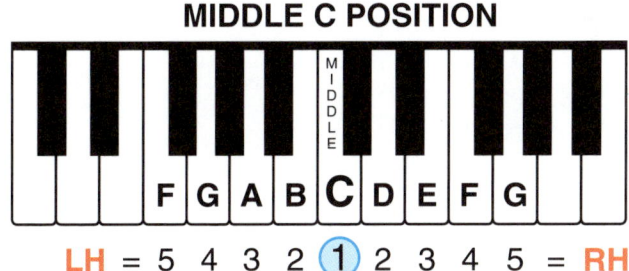

MIDDLE C POSITION

LH = 5 4 3 2 (1) 2 3 4 5 = RH

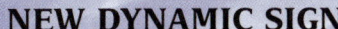

🔊 GM/CD 2-12 (53)

1. Let's go to the zoo, and you can see the tall gi - raffe.
2. We will see the chim - pan - zee, and bears and ti - gers too.

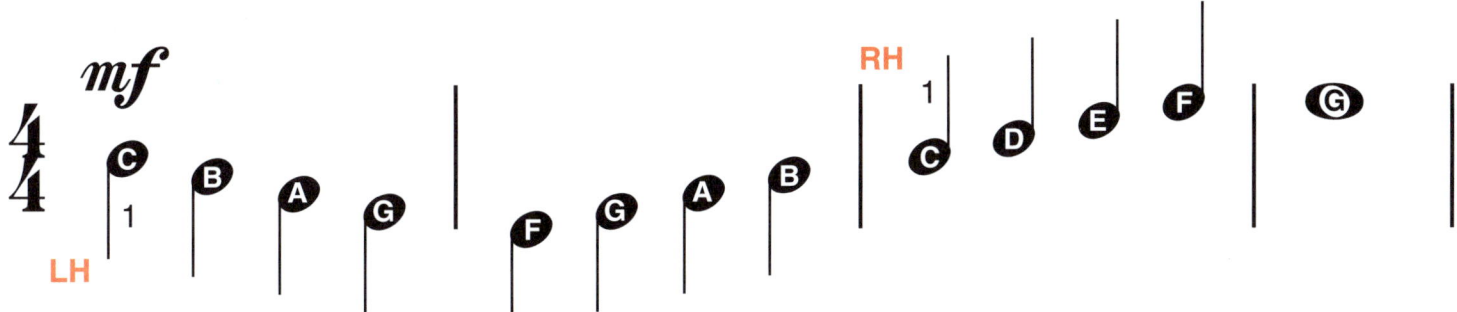

Mon - keys play - ing, swing - ing, sway - ing, al - ways make us laugh!
There is fun for ev - 'ry - one when we go to the zoo!

DUET PART (Student plays 1 octave higher.)

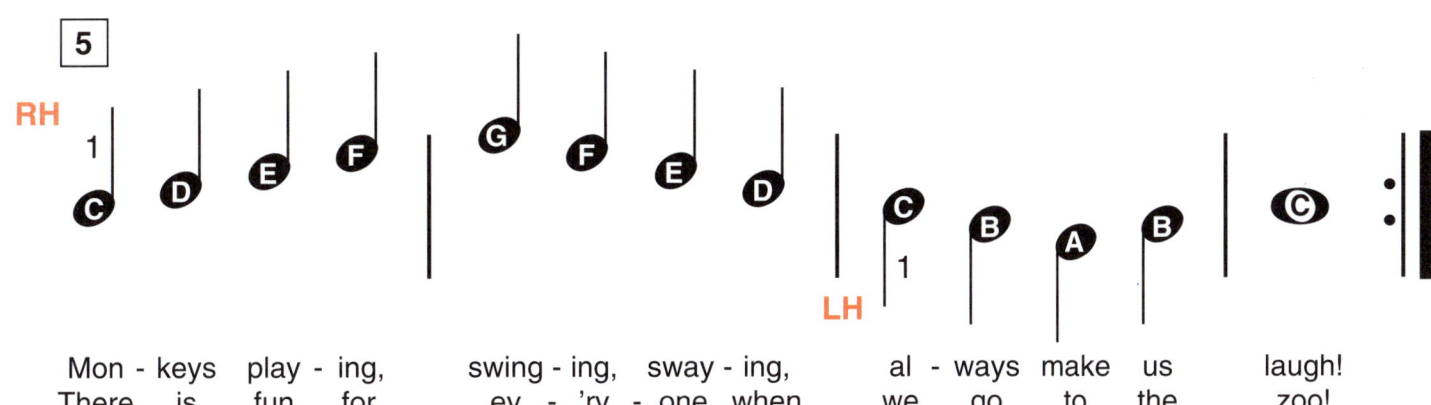

Ensemble PART 1

Lost My Partner!

MIDDLE C POSITION

GM/CD 2-13 (54)

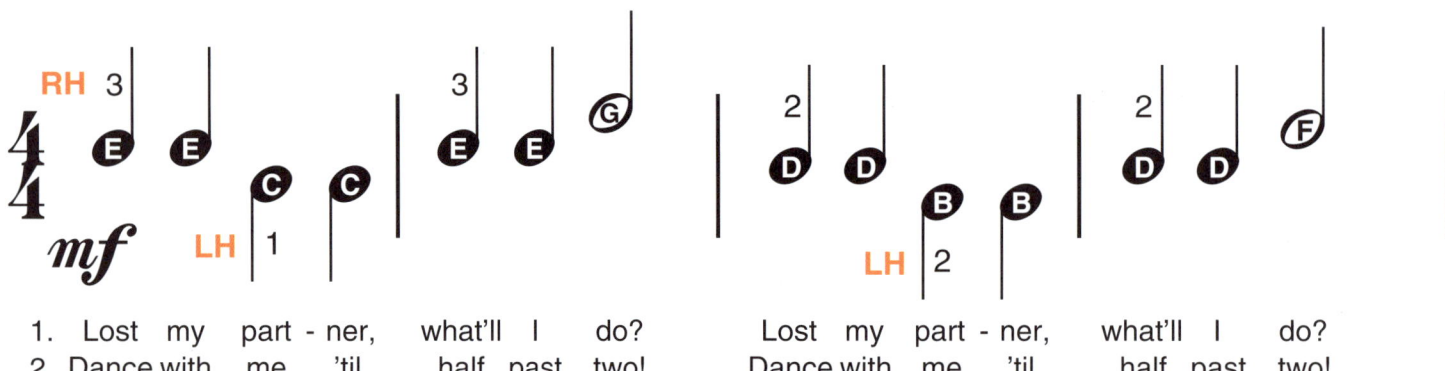

1. Lost my part - ner, what'll I do?
2. Dance with me 'til half past two!

Lost my part - ner, what'll I do?
Dance with me 'til half past two!

5

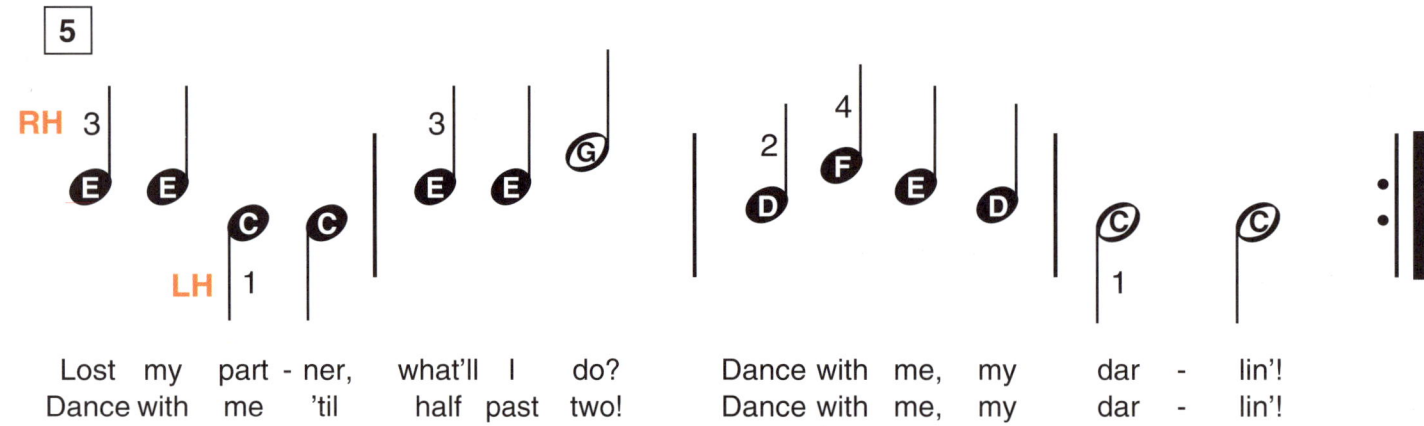

Lost my part - ner, what'll I do?
Dance with me 'til half past two!

Dance with me, my dar - lin'!
Dance with me, my dar - lin'!

TEACHER: See page 77.

Lost My Partner!

MIDDLE C POSITION

(Both hands 1 octave higher throughout)

🔊 GM/CD 2-13 (54)

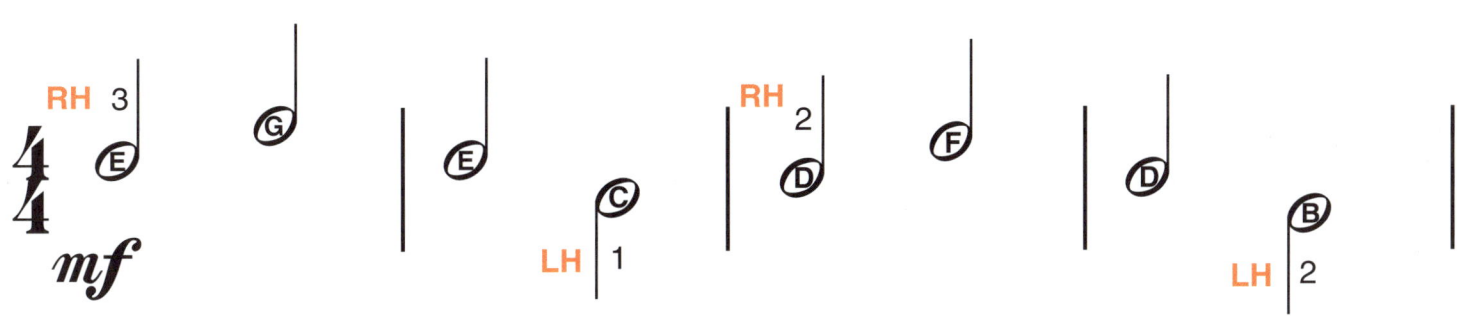

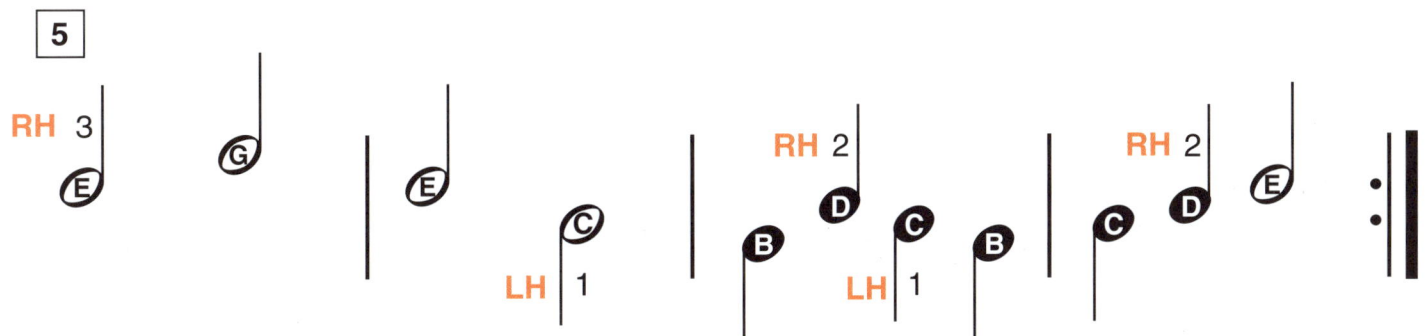

TEACHER: See page 77.

Lost My Partner!

MIDDLE C POSITION

(Both hands 1 octave lower throughout)

🔊))) GM/CD 2-13 (54)

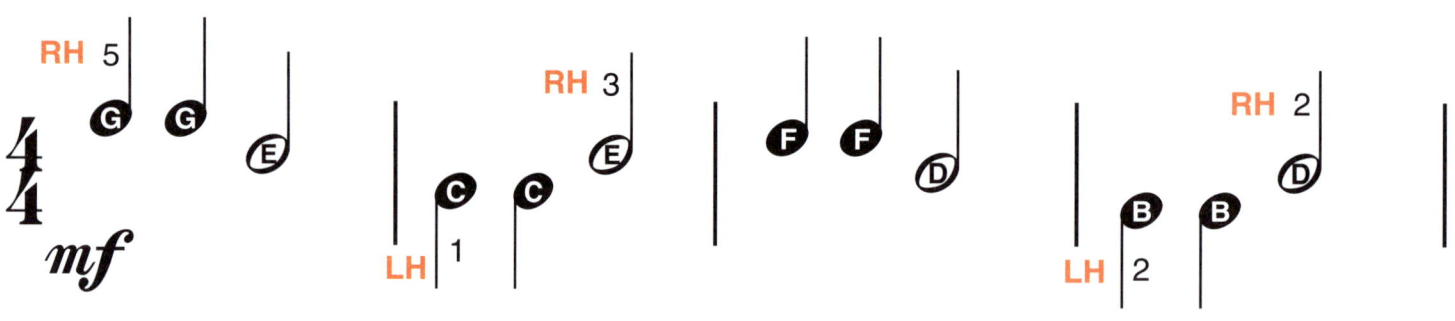

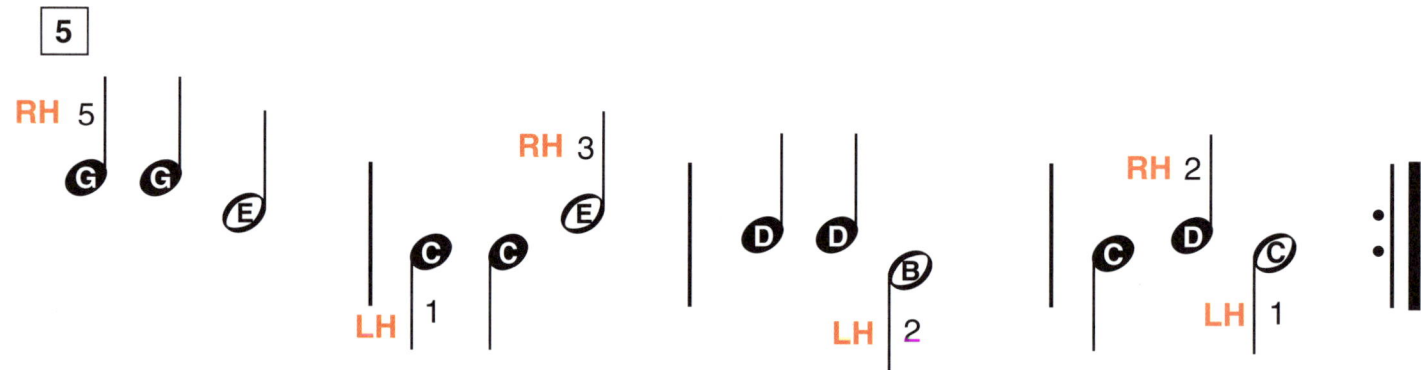

TEACHER: See page 77.

Lost My Partner!

MIDDLE C POSITION

(Both hands 1 octave lower throughout)

🔊))) GM/CD 2-13 (54)

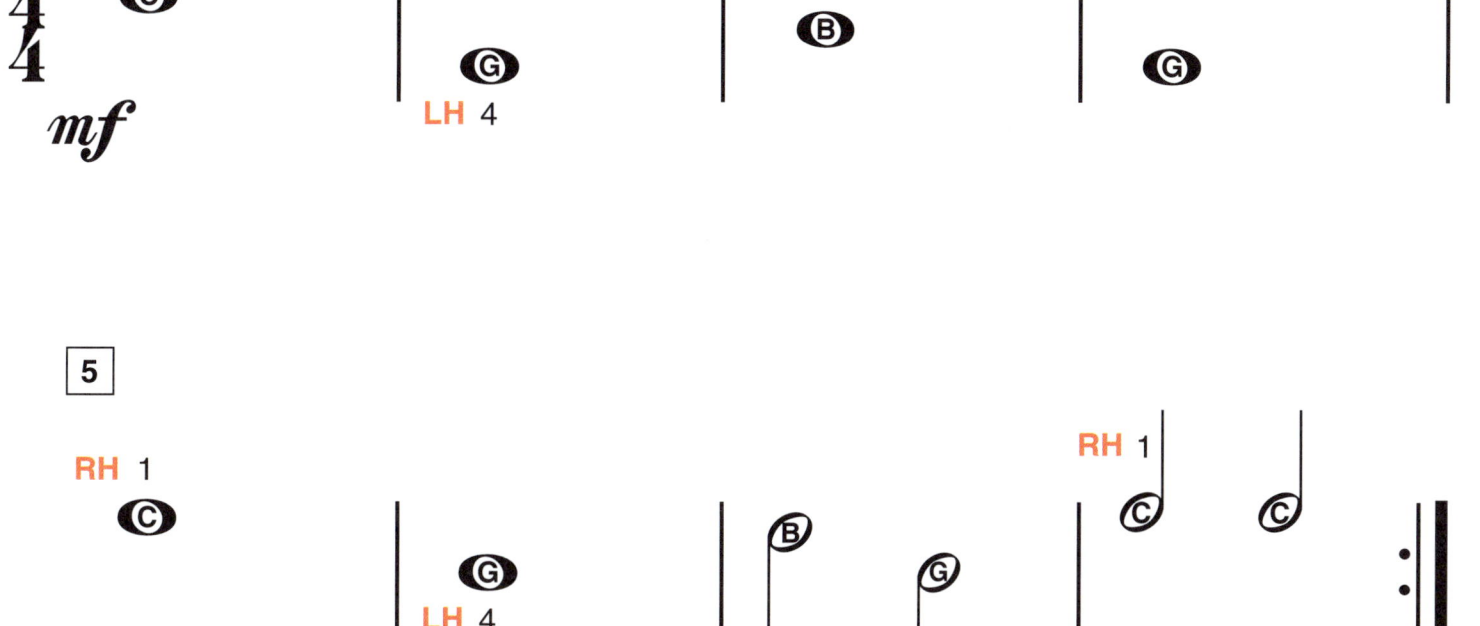

TEACHER: See page 77.

Playing in a New Position

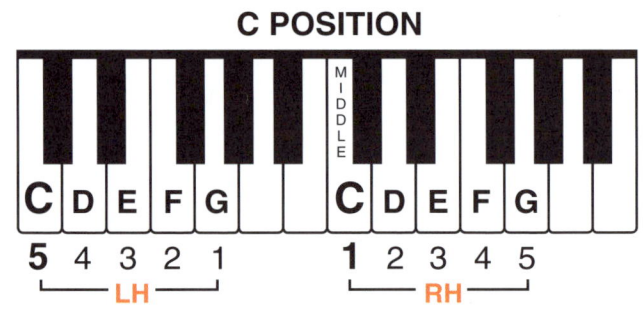

🔊 GM/CD 2-14 (55)

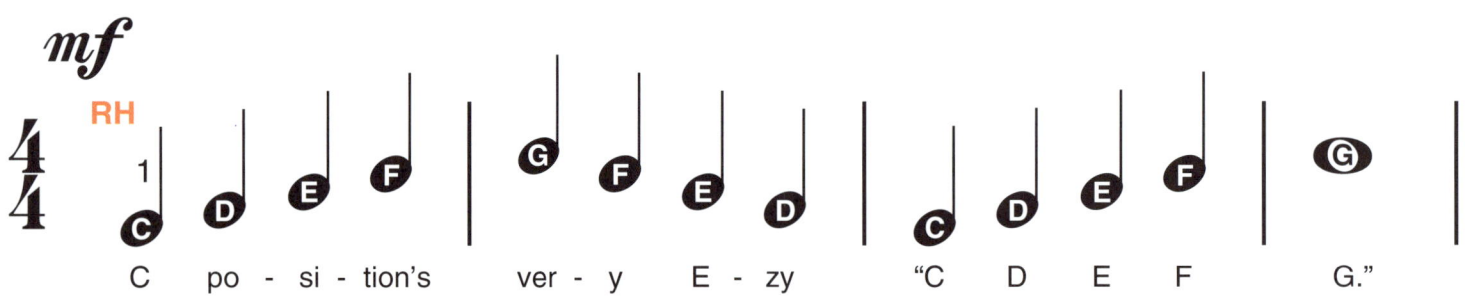

_mf_

RH

C po - si - tion's ver - y E - zy "C D E F G."

5

LH

Gee, I'm play - ing "C D E F G," as you can "C!"

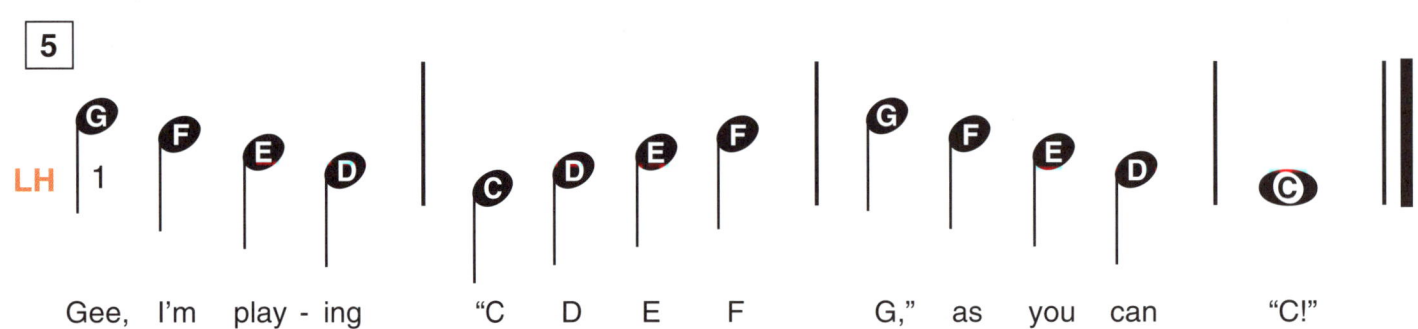

Technique

C POSITION

In each example below, play four ways:

1. Hands separately in C position.
2. RH, an octave higher.
3. LH, an octave lower.
4. Hands together.

Begin slowly and gradually play faster,
but always play EVENLY.

Keep fingers curved!

1st Team Warm-Up

Fingers 1, 2 & 3 are your STAR players!

🔊))) GM/CD 2-15 (56)

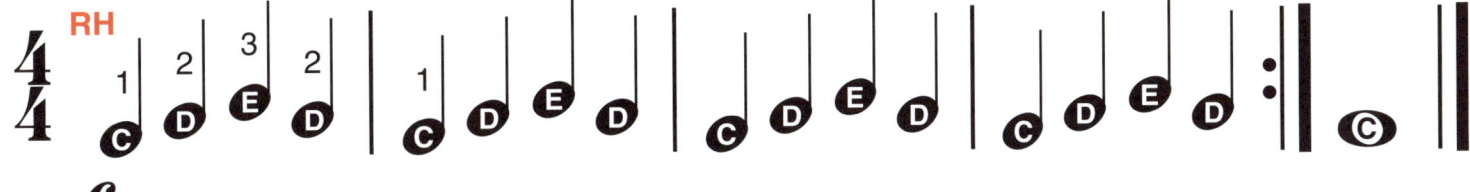

Initiation

The new player in this warm-up is finger 4.

🔊))) GM/CD 2-16 (57)

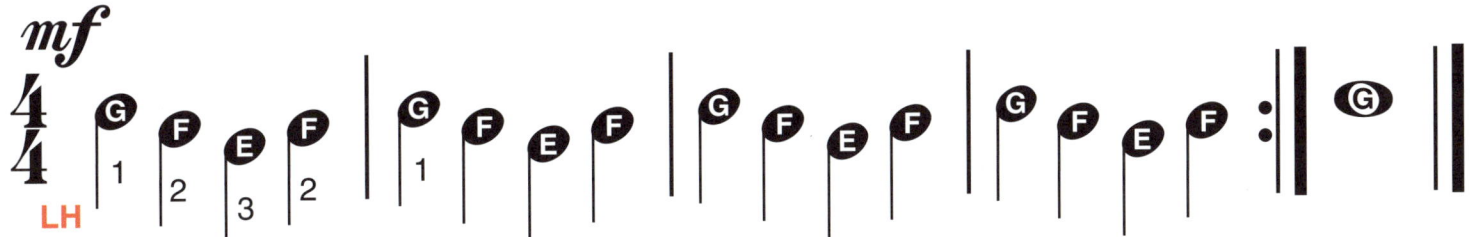

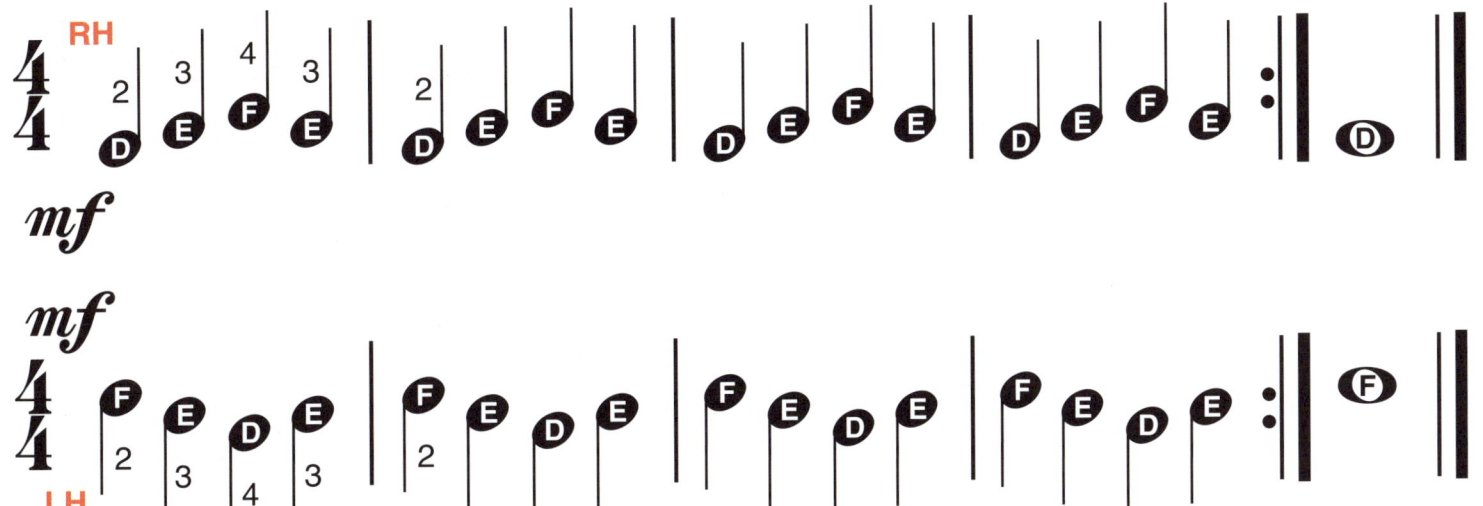

Theory

1. Draw lines connecting the dots to match the right hand finger number with the key that it plays in C POSITION.

RH 1 •

RH 2 •

RH 3 •

RH 4 •

RH 5 •

2. Draw lines connecting the dots to match the left hand finger number with the key that it plays in C POSITION.

LH 5 •

LH 4 •

LH 3 •

LH 2 •

LH 1 •

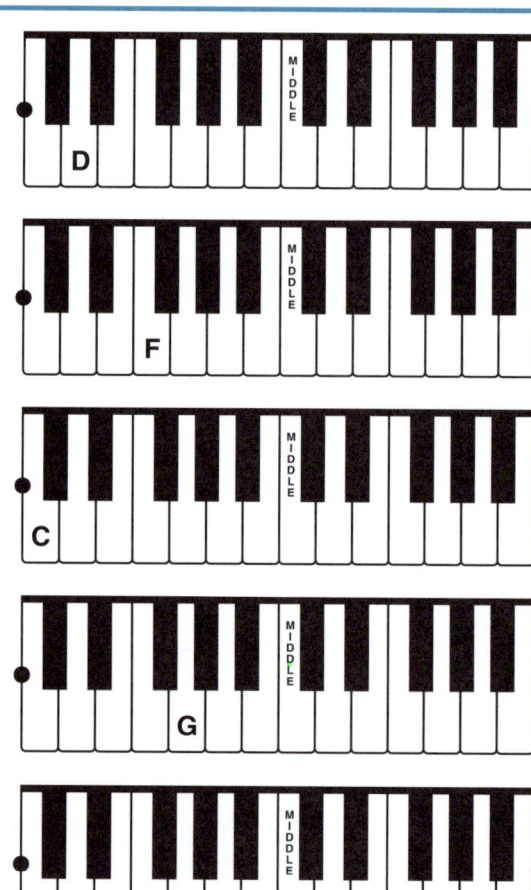

A New Time Signature

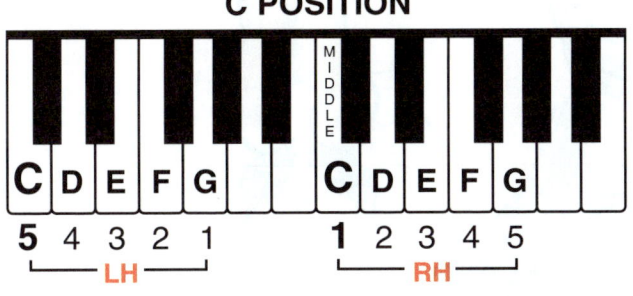

$\frac{3}{4}$ means **3** beats to each measure.

a **quarter note** gets one beat.

C POSITION

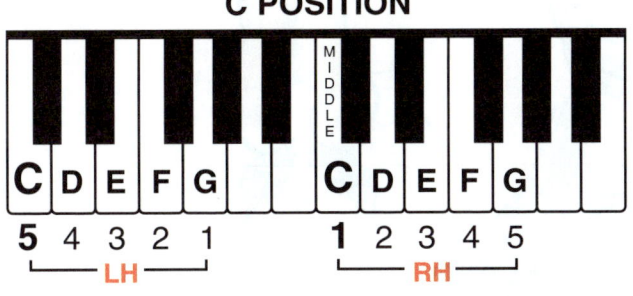

C D E F G   C D E F G

5 4 3 2 1   1 2 3 4 5

LH   RH

Dotted Half Note   a **longer** note.

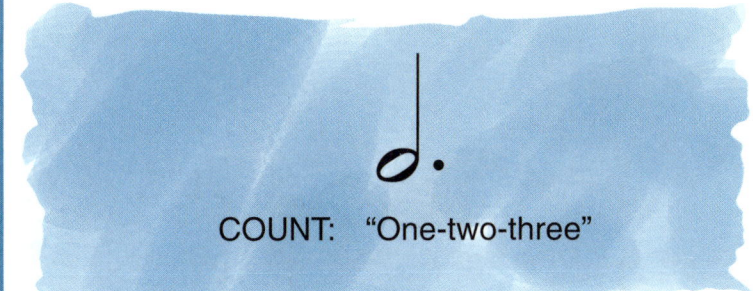

COUNT: "One-two-three"

1. Clap (or tap) the following rhythm.

2. Clap **ONCE** for each note, counting aloud as you clap.

Sailing

🔊 GM/CD 2-17 (58)

   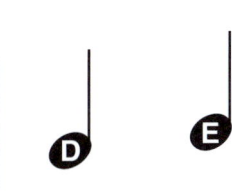  

RH 1

1. Come,   come,   come   to   the   sea!
2. Sea -   gulls   'round us   will   play.

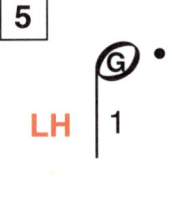    

5

LH 1

Come,   come,   sail - ing   with   me!
We'll   go   sail - ing   a   -   way.

DUET PART (Student plays 1 octave higher.)

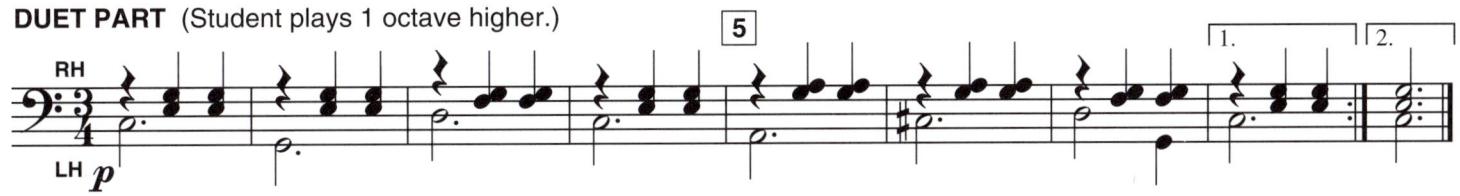

NOTE: You are now ready to play the game **Musical Adventures** (Rhythm Patterns and Terms & Symbols game cards)!

59

Skating

🔊 GM/CD 2-18 (59)

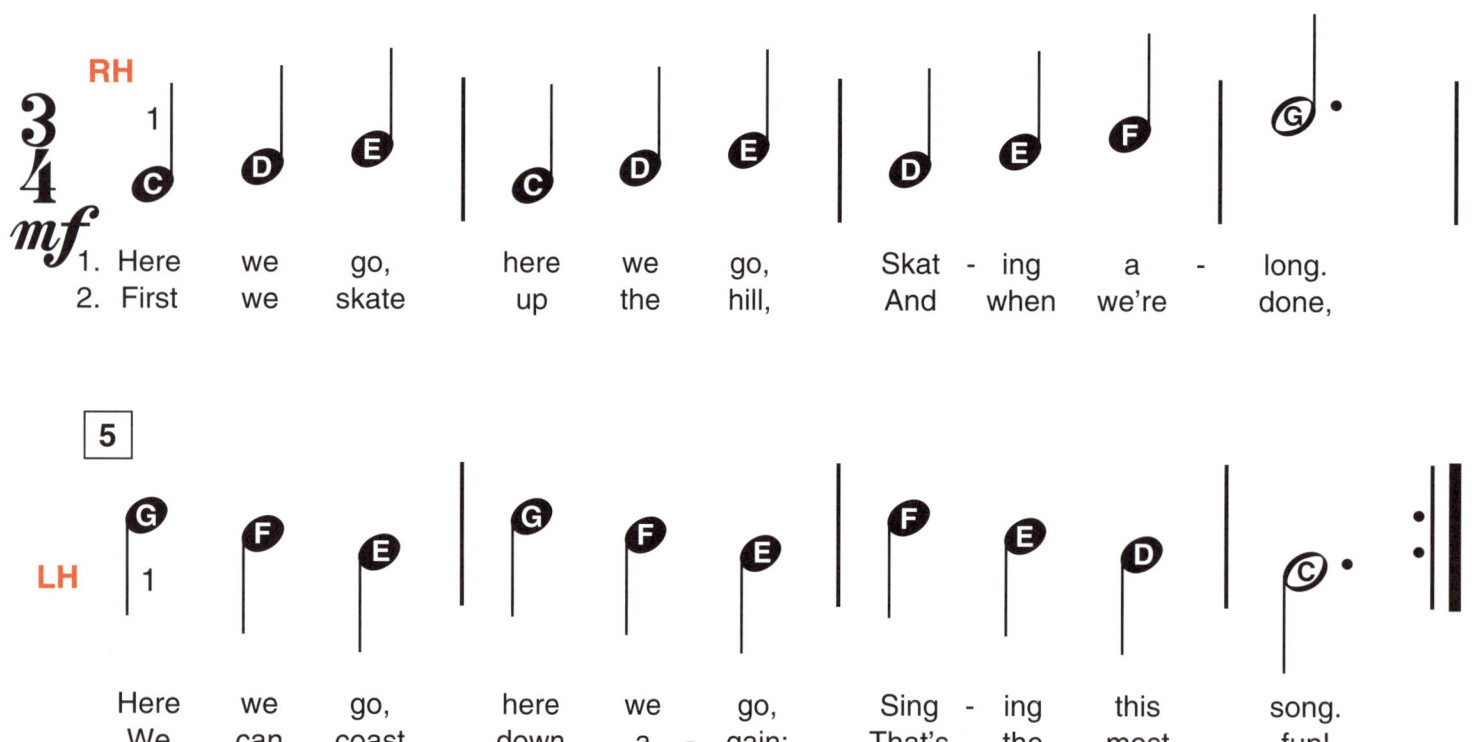

RH

$\frac{3}{4}$ **mf**

1. Here we go, here we go, Skat - ing a - long.
2. First we skate up the hill, And when we're done,

5

LH

Here we go, here we go, Sing - ing this song.
We can coast down a - gain; That's the most fun!

TEACHER'S NOTE: The DUET PART of SAILING (on page 59) may be played with SKATING.

The Dotted Half Note 𝅗𝅥.

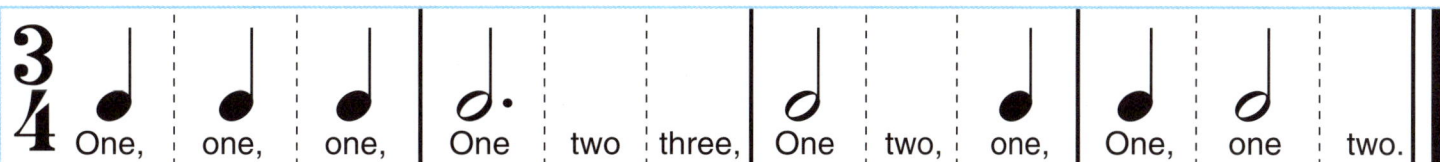

The notes in each measure must add up to 3 COUNTS!

1. After the **3/4** below, draw a DOTTED HALF NOTE over each "one."

2. Add BAR LINES. Put a DOUBLE BAR at the end.

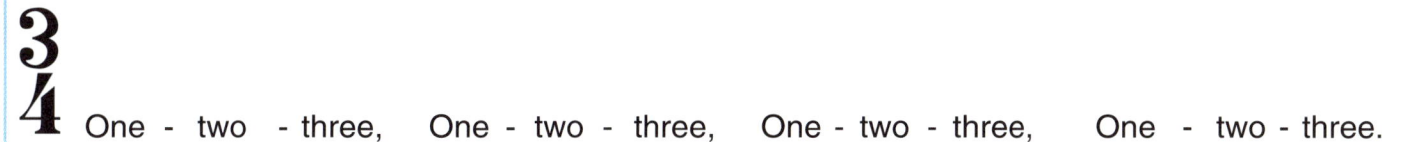

One - two - three,   One - two - three,   One - two - three,   One - two - three.

3. In the square below each note, write the number of counts it receives.

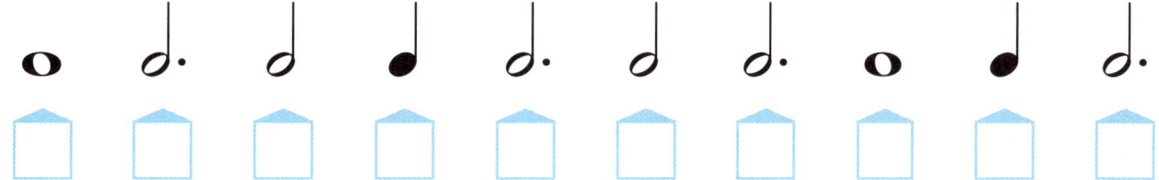

4. Under each line, write ONE NOTE equal in value to the sum of the TWO notes above it, as shown in the first example.

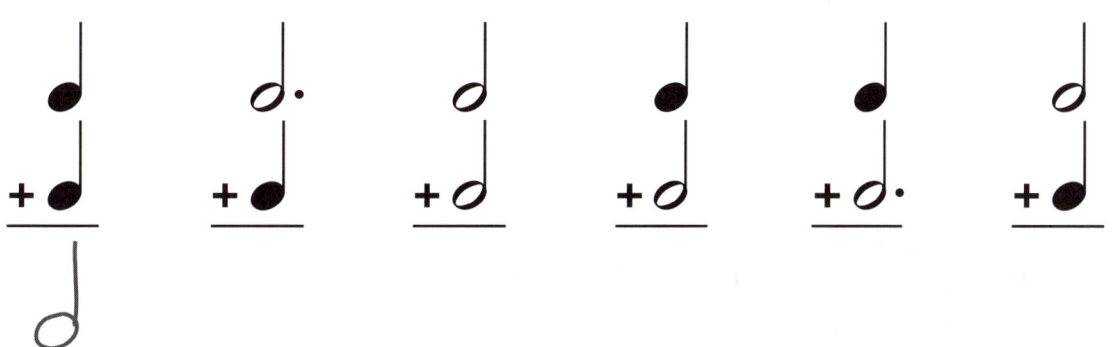

Technique

C POSITION

In each example below, play four ways:

1. Hands separately in C position.
2. RH, an octave higher.
3. LH, an octave lower.
4. Hands together.

Begin slowly and gradually play faster,
 but always play EVENLY.
Keep fingers curved!

My Turn!   Now it's time to add the fifth finger.

GM/CD 2-19 (60)

Everybody Play!

GM/CD 2-20 (61)

Quarter, Half and Dotted Half Notes

1. Your teacher will clap a rhythm pattern. Circle the pattern that you hear.

2. Your teacher will clap a rhythm pattern. Write the time signature and the pattern that you hear.

🔊 GM/CD 2-21 (62)

1a

1b

1c

1d

🔊 GM/CD 2-22 (63)

2a

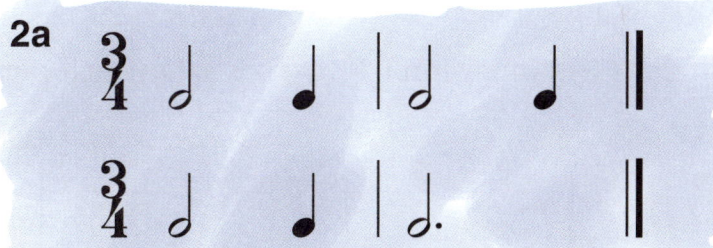

Pattern: _____

2b

Pattern: _____

2c

Pattern: _____

2d

Pattern: _____

TEACHER: See page 80.

Rhythm Drills

Clap (or tap) the following rhythms, counting aloud.

GM/CD 2-23 (64)

a.

GM/CD 2-24 (65)

b.

GM/CD 2-25 (66)

c.

Composition / Improvisation

1. Create melodies in the C position using the rhythm pattern below. Begin and end each hand with the given finger numbers.

2. Write the note name on the line below each note for your favorite melody.

3. Write a different dynamic sign (f, mf or p) in each box.

GM/CD 2-26 (67)

RH

C ___ ___ ___ ___ G

LH

G ___ ___ ___ ___ ___ C

Strange Lands

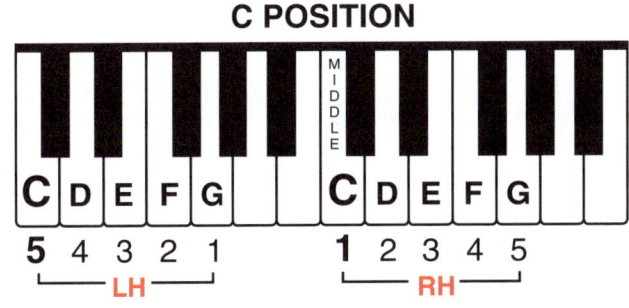

C POSITION

GM/CD 2-27 (68)

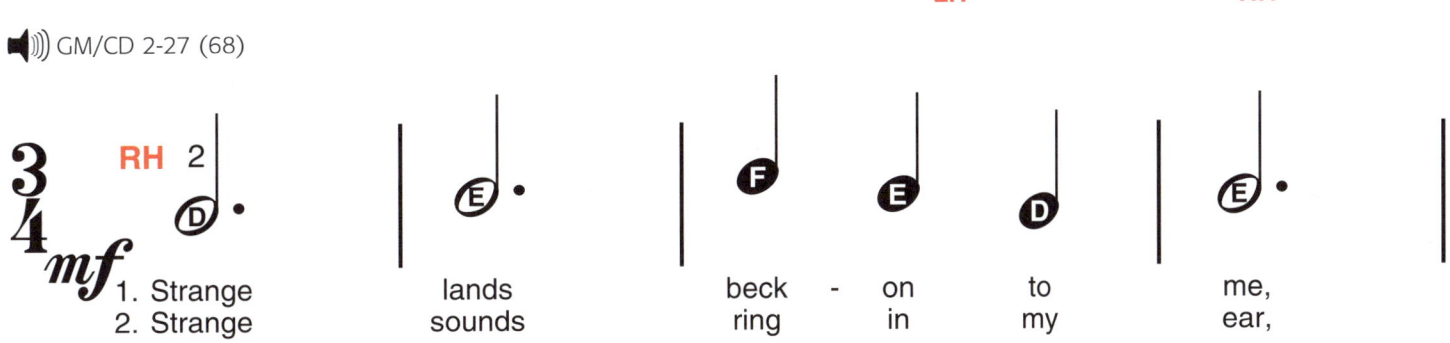

RH 2

$\frac{3}{4}$ *mf*

1. Strange   lands   beck - on   to   me,
2. Strange   sounds   ring   in   my   ear,

5

LH 3

Lands   I'm   long - ing   to   see.
Sounds   I'm   long - ing   to   hear.

Wishing Well

C POSITION

🔊))) GM/CD 2-28 (69)

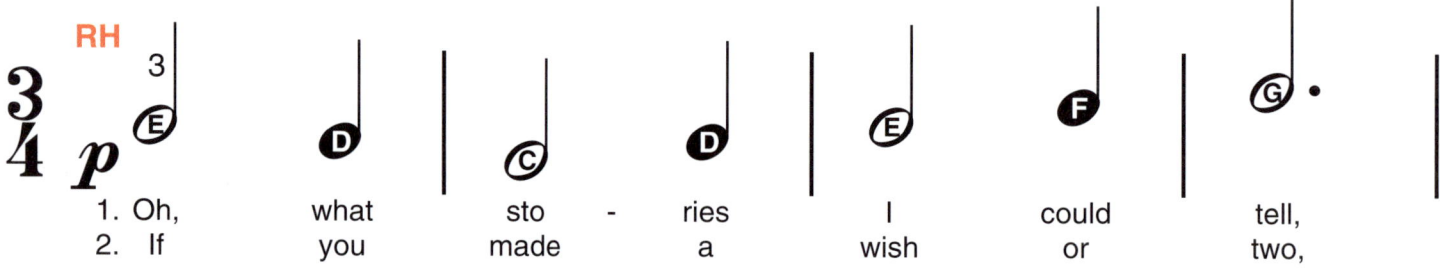

RH

3/4 *p*

	3 E	D	C	D	E	F	G·	

1. Oh, what sto - ries I could tell,
2. If you made a wish or two,

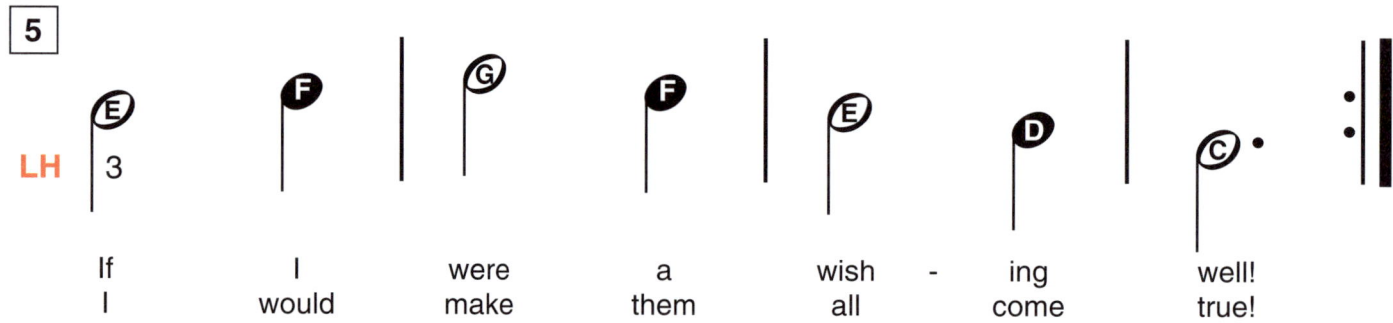

5

LH 3

E	F	G	F	E	D	C·	

If I were a wish - ing well!
I would make them all come true!

DUET PART (Student plays 1 octave higher.)

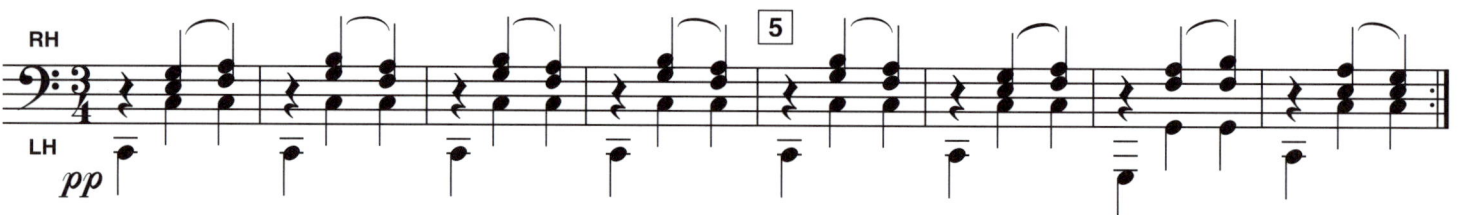

RH 9:3/4

LH *pp*

66

Sight Reading

1. Clap (or tap) & count.
2. Play finger numbers in the air & count.
3. Play & count.
4. Play & say note names.

GM/CD 2-29 (70)

a. $\frac{3}{4}$ LH **mf** — F(2), E, D, C.

  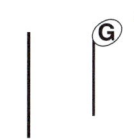

GM/CD 2-30 (71)

b. $\frac{3}{4}$ LH **f** — G(1), F, E, G.

 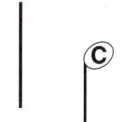

GM/CD 2-31 (72)

c. $\frac{3}{4}$ LH **p** — E(3), E, D, C.

GM/CD 2-32 (73)

d. $\frac{3}{4}$ RH **p** — C(1), D, E, C.

GM/CD 2-33 (74)

e. $\frac{3}{4}$ RH **f** — D(2), E, F, G.

GM/CD 2-34 (75)

f. $\frac{3}{4}$ RH **mf** — F(4), G, F, E.

Rhythm Drills

Clap (or tap) the following rhythms, counting aloud.

🔊 GM/CD 2-35 (76)

a.

🔊 GM/CD 2-36 (77)

b.

🔊 GM/CD 2-37 (78)

c.

1. Create melodies in the C position using the rhythm pattern below. Begin and end with the given finger numbers.

2. Write the note name on the line below each note for your favorite melody.

3. Write a different dynamic sign (f , mf or p) in each box.

🔊 GM/CD 2-38 (79)

RH

$\frac{3}{4}$ 1   C

LH

5   C

Ear Training

Rhythm Patterns

1. Your teacher will clap two rhythm patterns.

   • Circle SAME if the patterns are the SAME.
   • Circle DIFFERENT if the patterns are DIFFERENT.

2. Your teacher will clap a rhythm pattern.
   Circle the pattern that you hear.

🔊 GM/CD 2-39 (80)

1a SAME different

1b SAME different

1c SAME different

1d SAME different

🔊 GM/CD 2-40 (81)

2a

2b

2c

2d

TEACHER: See page 80.

What Can I Share?

C POSITION

GM/CD 2-41 (82)

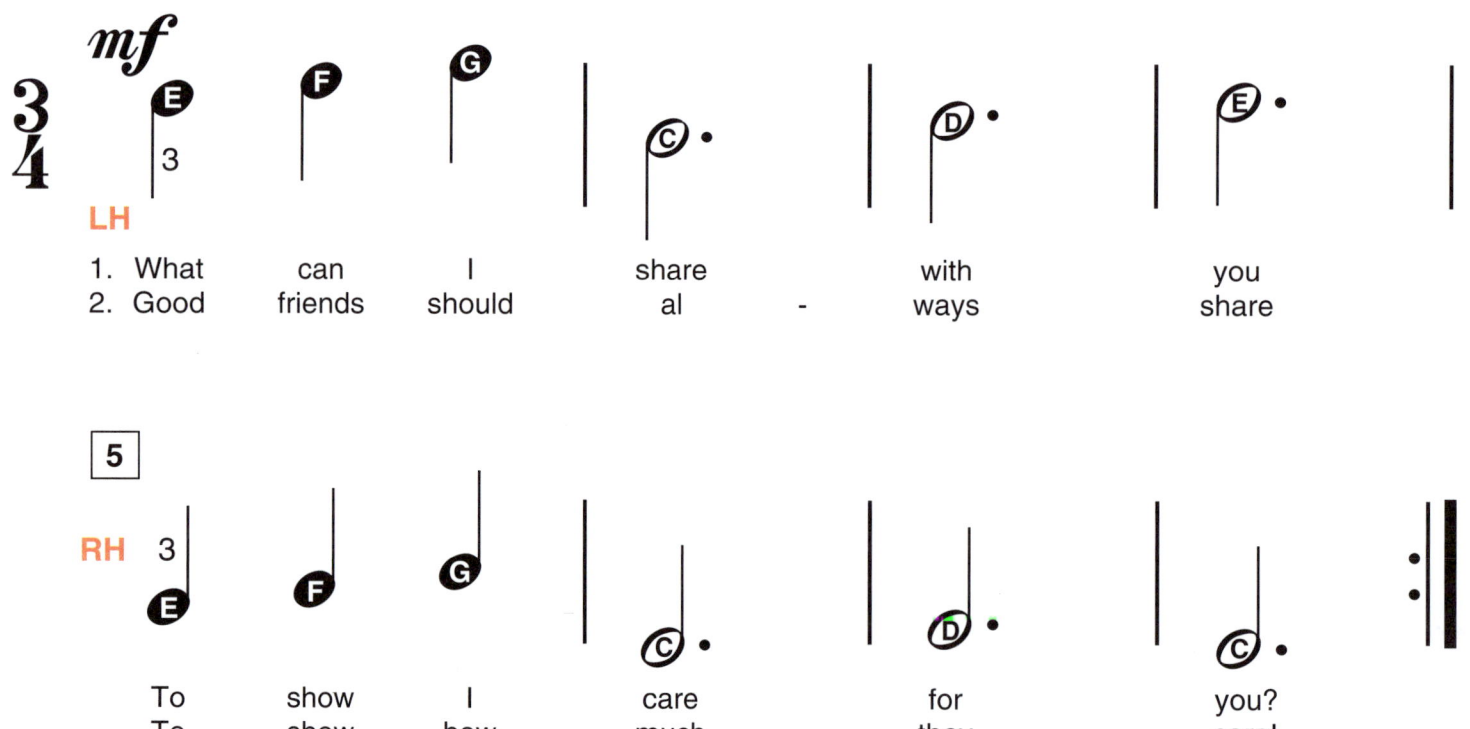

mf

3/4

LH

1. What can I share with you
2. Good friends I should al - ways share

5

RH

To show I care for you?
To show how much they care!

TEACHER: See page 78.

What Can I Share?

C POSITION
(Both hands 1 octave higher throughout)

GM/CD 2-41 (82)

TEACHER: See page 78.

What Can I Share?

C POSITION
(Both hands 1 octave higher throughout)

🔊)) GM/CD 2-41 (82)

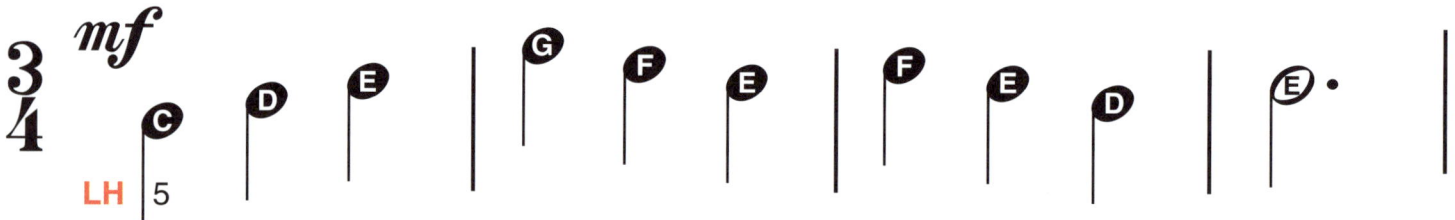

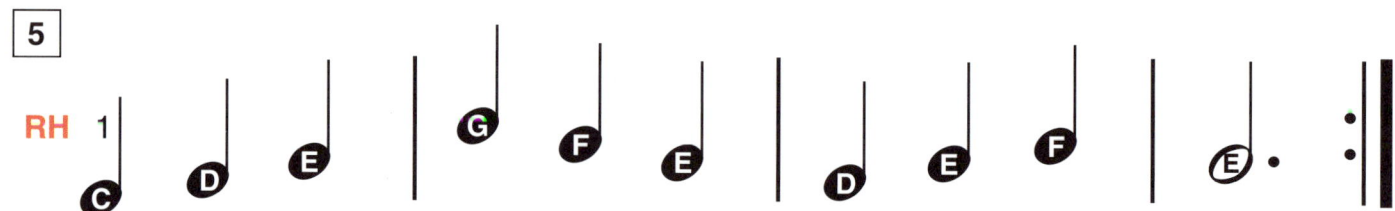

TEACHER: See page 78.

What Can I Share?

C POSITION
(Both hands 1 octave lower throughout)

🔊 GM/CD 2-41 (82)

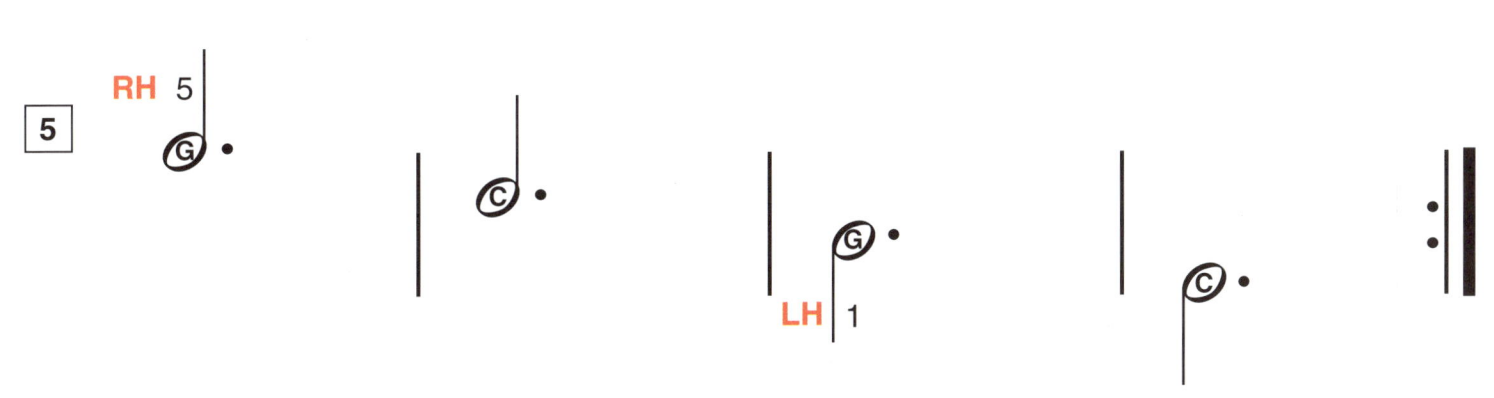

TEACHER: See page 78.

Theory

| *mf* | ♩ (half note) | **3/4** | *p* | 𝅝 (whole note) | *f* | ♩ (quarter note) | ♩. (dotted half note) |

Write each of the above signs in the correct squares below.
Write each sign TWICE; once in the LEFT column and once in the RIGHT column.

☐	piano	☐	count 4 for this note.
☐	dotted half note	☐	loud
☐	time signature	☐	count 2 for this note.
☐	quarter note	☐	means there are 3 counts in each measure.
☐	mezzo forte	☐	soft
☐	whole note	☐	count 1 for this note.
☐	half note	☐	moderately loud
☐	forte	☐	count 3 for this note.

Certificate of Promotion

This is to certify that

_____

has successfully completed

Alfred's Basic Piano Library
Group Piano Course, Book 1

and is hereby promoted to

Alfred's Basic Piano Library
Group Piano Course, Book 2.

_____

Date

_____

Teacher

Sailor Jack

GM/CD 1-39 (83)
BLACK KEY POSITION

Lyrics (part 1-2):
1. Sail - or Jack, where have you been? 'Round the world and back a - gain!
2. When will you be sail - ing back? Soon as moth - er packs my sack!

Lyrics (part 5):
Sail - or Jack, how did you sail? Rode u - pon a hump - back whale!
How'll you sail back Sail - or Jack? In my dad's new Cad - il - lac!

Student pages 30–33.

Lost My Partner!

GM/CD 2-13 (54)
MIDDLE C POSITION

Lyrics (verse 1 & 2):
1. Lost my part-ner, what'll I do? Lost my part-ner, what'll I do?
2. Dance with me 'til half past two! Dance with me 'til half past two!

Section 5:
Lost my part-ner, what'll I do? Dance with me, my dar-lin'!
Dance with me 'til half past two! Dance with me, my dar-lin'!

Student pages 52-55.

TEACHER'S EXAMPLES

What Can I Share?

Student pages 70-73.

Page 9 (Play)

GM/CD 1-1 (45)

1a.

b.

c.

d.

GM/CD 1-2 (46)

2a.

b.

c.

d.

Page 16 (Clap)

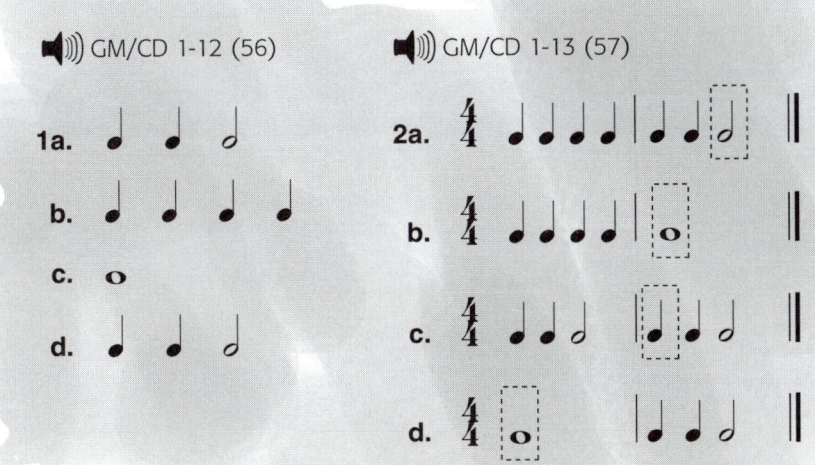

GM/CD 1-12 (56)

1a.

b.

c.

d.

GM/CD 1-13 (57)

2a.

b.

c.

d.

Page 28 (Clap)

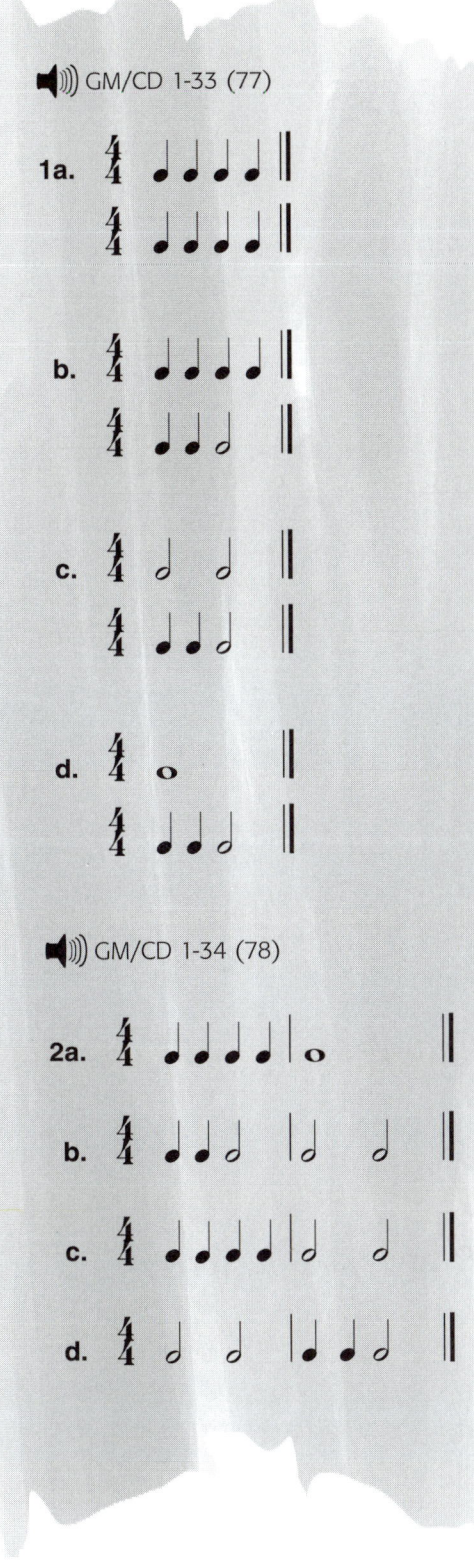

GM/CD 1-33 (77)

1a.

b.

c.

d.

GM/CD 1-34 (78)

2a.

b.

c.

d.

Page 49 (Play)

Page 69 (Clap)

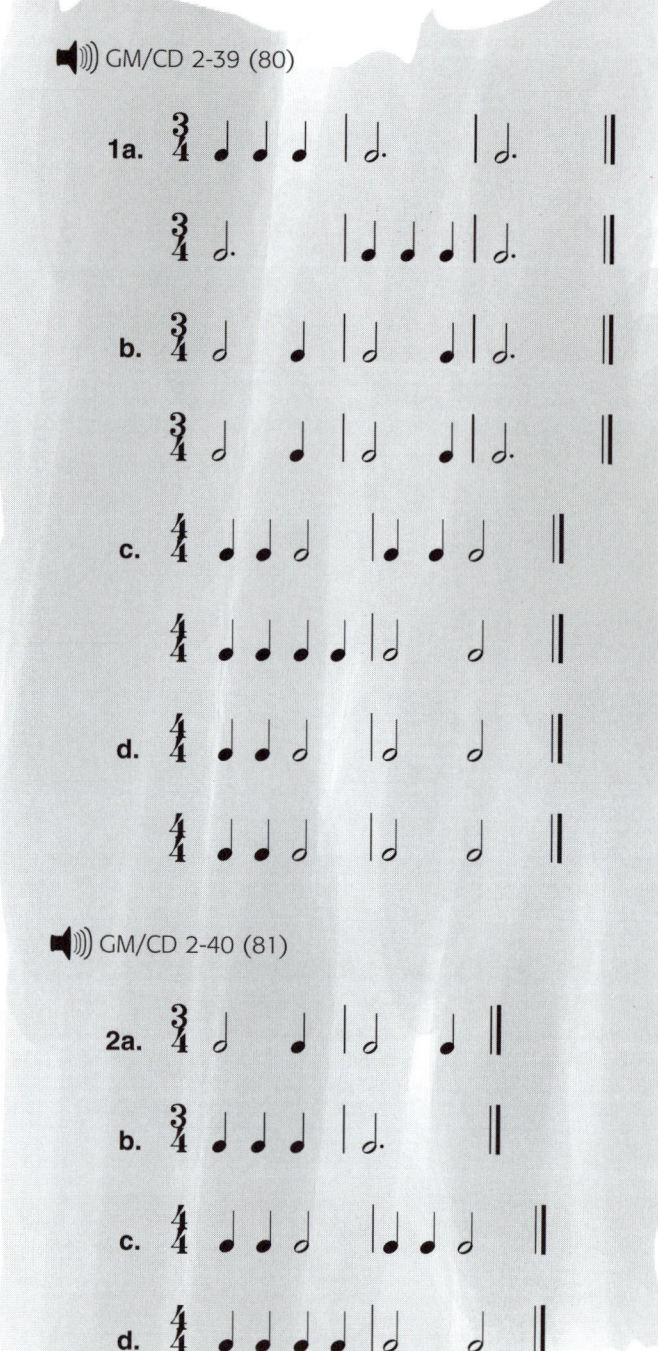

Page 63 (Clap)

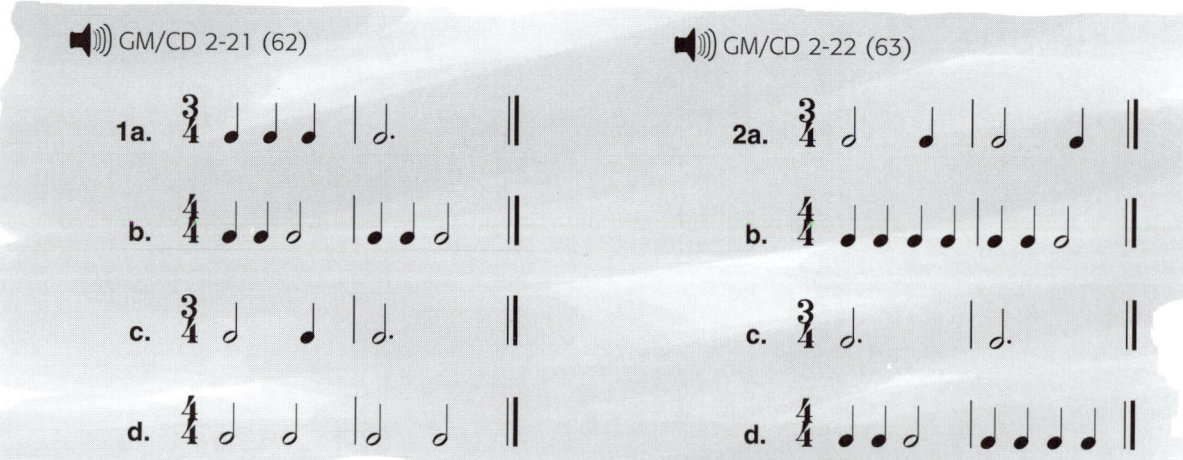